T0208542

MY GOD'S MERCY,
NOW THAT I THINK ABOUT IT!

LILLIE V. APIYO

WestBow
PRESS
A DIVISION OF THOMAS NELSON

All scripture references are taken from the King James Version of the Holy Bible

WestBow Press books may be ordered through booksellers or by contacting:

WestBow Press
A Division of Thomas Nelson
1663 Liberty Drive
Bloomington, IN 47403
www.westbowpress.com
1 (866) 928-1240

ISBN: 978-1-4908-1138-3 (sc)
ISBN: 978-1-4908-1137-6 (hc)
ISBN: 978-1-4908-1139-0 (e)

Library of Congress Control Number: 2013918441

Printed in the United States of America.

WestBow Press rev. date: 10/18/2013

CONTENTS

CONTENTS

DEDICATION

This book is dedicated to my Lord and Savior, Jesus Christ, for it is He who empowered me to write the book; my children: Charlene, Russell, Jason, Jarome, Lili, and Tafton Miller, and Shuntaye Simmons; surviving relatives of the late Pastor Lillie B. Sanlin, and the Faith Temple Pentecostal Church Family.

ACKNOWLEDGMENTS

Nathan McDonald, Thank you for critiquing the manuscript and serving as mentor on this writing project. You were so instrumental and I appreciate you!

Monica Harris and Florence Cocroft, Thank you for critiquing the manuscript as well. I will not forget the kindness shown.

Evangelist Delois Kennedy, Your encouragement and assistance in helping to jog my memory has been priceless. Thanks for the prayers and suggestions. You are a blessing.

Pastor Darrell Peavy, Your constant reminder to complete the book worked. Thanks for the prayers and all assistance given.

Eliza Thomas, Thank you for all suggestions given to help "perk-up" the book.

The Faith Temple family, Thank you for your prayers and words of encouragement.

INTRODUCTION

How often has the Lord extended mercy unto us and we simply overlooked it? Perhaps you can relate to instances when you did not comprehend just what was going on in the spiritual realm. Why did things develop as they did? This was not the scenario you imagined in your mind. The odds were against you and even the outcome was surprising! God was surrounding you with His mercy (compassion), even when you were not aware of His presence in the midst of that situation. Angels were on assignment from the Lord and things worked out in your favor.

That is what *My God's Mercy (Now That I Think About It!)* endeavors to portray. It is a brief reflection of how God's compassion was revealed to me. The book contains true stories that begin with family, and people strategically placed in my life by God, to bring change, naturally and spiritually. Every effort has been made to assure the accuracy of events or dates given. The late Pastor Lillie B. Sanlin is interwoven throughout the book, as she was one of the "vessels of honor" God used to introduce me to new life in Jesus.

As I reflect on the past, embrace the present-day, and get excited about future possibilities, I know assuredly that God has shown Himself mighty on my behalf. Trace my journey carefully and see the Hand of God at work so that He gets my attention and the glory.

This writing project began in 1973. I was led of the Spirit to write a book regarding the ministry of the late Evangelist Lillie B. Sanlin, founder and pastor of the Faith Temple Pentecostal Church Mission, Incorporated, Kosciusko, Mississippi. I had no idea that twenty years later I would serve as pastor of that same ministry!

I had only written about five pages of the manuscript when I showed Pastor Sanlin my small beginnings. She was pleased that I wanted to honor her by writing a book about her life and ministry.

However, procrastination and the cares of this life including marriage, children, and full time employment, crept in. The project ceased and lay dormant inside a folder in the bedroom closet. The flame I once had for writing a book began dwindling, and was eventually reduced to only a spark. Periodically, the Lord would remind me of the incomplete project, and I would write a few more pages and add them to the folder.

In 1976 our family relocated to Harvey, Louisiana. On February 16, 1983, the Lord called Pastor Sanlin to rest from her labors. I was contacted by the program committee regarding my writing project. The committee wanted to review my information for possible inclusion in the obituary. I submitted it and some was actually used.

After Pastor Sanlin's home-going celebration I felt as though I had failed, because I had purposed to write my book during her lifetime. Nevertheless, God was still merciful, and a few years later he began to renew my desire for writing. So I wrote a few more pages and added them to that special folder.

Many years have passed and I have no more excuses to give myself, people, or the Lord (in reference to completing the writing project). So here I go, writing once more. Only this time I am removing pages from that folder, fine tuning them and placing them in alignment for the manuscript. This latest nudge from the Holy Ghost caused me to make a commitment to complete the project. Yes, "I can do all things through Christ that strengtheth me." (Phillipians 4:13)

The name of the Lord is exalted as God's mercy comes into fruition bringing testimonies of salvation, divine healing, and deliverance from demonic oppression.

Luke, the beloved physician, informs us of the following scenario involving Jesus, "And as He entered into a certain village there met Him ten men that were lepers, which stood afar off: and they lifted up their voices and said, Jesus, Master, have mercy on us." (Luke 17:12-13)

The lepers, persons suffering from leprosy, cried out to Jesus, desiring mercy in the form of cleansing, deliverance from their leprous condition. Leprosy is a contagious disease that affects the skin, mucous membrane, and nerves, causing discoloration, and lumps on the skin, and in severe cases, disfigurement, and deformities. Hansen's disease. (Kindle-New Oxford American Dictionary, second edition)

Jesus did not even pray for the lepers. Instead, He instructed them to go show themselves to the priest. The scripture states that as they went (traveled), they (the lepers) were cleansed. One leper took note of his healing. Rather than continue his trip, and be pronounced cleansed of the leprosy by the priests, he turned around. The former leper found Jesus, and said, (paraphrased) "Thank you Lord! Thank you Lord!" Now all ten men had been healed, but only one returned to express gratitude for the compassion Jesus had shown. (Luke 17:14-18)

Take a few minutes and think about how God's mercy has prevailed in your life. Now, tell the Lord "Thank you Jesus!" for He has been, and still is good to you.

Like King David, we too can say, "O give thanks unto the Lord; for He is good: and His mercy endureth forever." (Psalms 136:1)

MOMMA

ANNIE CATHERINE VEASLEY THOMPSON-LONDON
1923 – 1985

I was so privileged and blessed by God to have Annie Catherine Veasley as my mother. She was the daughter of Lillie Veasley and Dave Riley, born January 14, 1923.

By the time I was born (June 23, 1952) Momma was a single parent, although she had been married to Lar C Thompson and Eddie London. The odds were against her but she raised her children (Dorothy, James, Sara, Mary, Annie, Lillie, Alvin, and Robert) to the best of her ability. There were times I called her Mother, Mom, or Momma. Momma was short, pleasantly plump, brown facial complexion with a beautiful smile, affectionate eyes, and strong loving hands.

Momma could take a little and stretch it so far because she leaned heavily on the Lord. I often heard her singing "The Lord will make a way somehow, when beneath the cross I bow; so I say to my soul, don't you worry, no. The Lord will make a way somehow." That was her song of consolation by Thomas A. Dorsey, because whether happy or in the midst of turmoil, she could count on God to provide for her needs.

At an early age that song was deeply-rooted in my spirit as I witnessed Momma's great strength that came from the Lord. It was much later in life, when I too realized that even in the midst of turmoil; I could always count on God's provision and mercy to see me through. I was fortunate to grow up in rural Attala County under her watchful eye. Momma loved her children! Why I did not even know the meaning of the word "poor," as defined by living accommodations until I was in junior high school (1966). It was then that I had that rude awakening.

Our regular bus driver picked us up that morning, but in the afternoon he did not drive his route. This change caused us to be situated on another bus. As the bus approached our house some of the teenagers started laughing, and pointing. They said our house looked like "The fall of the Roman Empire." The teenagers were comparing our house to the ruins in the city of Rome after it was destroyed.

What they did not know was that the organized piles of iron, bean poles, tin cans, and redeemable glass soda bottles that were located near the side of the house were part of our home business. Momma sold those items when enough accumulated, and the cash was used to help pay bills. We had no running water, so several fifty gallon drums were positioned near the side of the house so that when it rained, water would run into the barrels. This water was sometimes used for washing clothes by hand and dishes. We walked to the nearby spring daily to get water for cooking, drinking, bathing and other needs.

Then for a brief moment it dawned on me, we must be "poor." For a while the thought of being poor seemed embarrassing. Then the revelation came and I moved on with my life. I realized that Momma was so busy providing for us that what we lacked in material things was made up for in love.

We were taught to never make fun of anyone without serious consequences following. If one of your siblings got a whipping and you were caught laughing, you got a whipping too. Talking back, being disrespectful or listening to "grown folks" conversations were not tolerated. Momma didn't play like that. A child stayed in a child's place, and that was reinforced. Now-a-days, we really need the Lord's help, because you sometimes wonder which the parent is and which is the child. Momma also taught us to be honest, as well as the importance of working for a living.

Momma did not have a car so she depended on others for transportation. We usually walked to town on Saturdays which was about three miles one way. Then we would get a ride back home with the grocery delivery man, or someone else we knew who was also in town.

When we could not get a ride to church, (Traveler's Rest Missionary Baptist Church), Momma would send us walking the three mile trip. After church someone would usually give us a ride back home. We would use our "every day shoes" for the walk, and carry our "church shoes" in a bag. Before getting too close to the church we would stop and change shoes. We would quickly shine our shoes with a left over biscuit from breakfast. It was important to us that our patent leather shoes shined like the other girls who did not have to walk to church.

Momma believed in God and you were going to church even when she could not make it. Thank God for Momma and her convictions! She was serious about guiding her children in the right way. As King Solomon stated, "Train up a child in the way he should go: and when he is old, he will not depart from it." (Proverbs 22:6)

Momma started developing my secretarial skills at an early age. When James and Sara moved out of state she would dictate letters to me, and I would write what she wanted to say.

She believed in being committed, whether it was a task at hand or a relationship. Teenagers were known to "play the field" by having more than one girlfriend or boyfriend, but not so in our house. You only dated one person. Only one was coming to visit (court) and you better not try to trick her. I thought Momma was being cruel, but I thank God that I learned commitment early in life. It was embedded in my character so I had no problem being faithful in marriage.

During my high school senior year (May 1970), when most graduates were having their boyfriends or girlfriends write on their "special" page, I asked Momma to do so. Now I had a boyfriend, Clarence Lewis, and he wrote on another page, but for some reason I wanted my mother to use that special page. Below is what she had to say taken from my senior memory book and it is my most prized possession.

"Dear Lillie,

You is the baby girl and I'm very proud of you for the way you helt out and finished school and I hope you continue to be good by the help of the Lord and gow to chuch and be some body. I hope so that all, May God blest you."

Mother,

Annie C. London

Momma was an advocate of education, and she wanted her children to have better education than what she received. I was going to be in school unless I was actually sick. Playing or pretending to be sick did not work with Momma.

Among my siblings, I was the first to graduate high school. My college education consisted of attending night classes' part time (1987-2005) at Magnolia Bible College, Kosciusko, Mississippi. In 2006 I transferred to Holmes Community College, Goodman, Mississippi, (night classes part time) and received an Associate of Arts Degree in General College Studies in May 2008. As I continue my educational quest, I will always be reminded of Momma's desire that her children and offspring would get a good education.

When my first child, Charlene, was born, I wanted to experience "Natural child birth" and Momma was right there for me (at her home). Going to Momma's house for this milestone in my life was really special. During this time it was not uncommon for mothers to deliver their babies at home under the care of a Mid-wife. The attending Mid-wife for my children delivered at home, Mrs. Lue Willie Bentley, knew her job would be less complicated with my mother present.

When Russell was born (natural childbirth as well) Momma was still there. He was born in her home also.

During my third pregnancy I was living in Harvey, Louisiana, but came home for the delivery around my sixth month due to marital problems. I was not aware that I was pregnant with twins, but Momma had mentioned the possibility of such. That had been my easiest pregnancy, and the labor period was so short that I could not make it to the hospital as planned. Instead, Momma delivered those babies at her house while my brother, Alvin, went to pick up Mrs. Bentley. All I can say is, "Wow, what a woman!"

I always believed my mother could handle anything because she exhibited so much strength in the midst of difficulties. Momma knew God was the source of her strength, and that His grace and mercy would be with her through every challenge. She left a godly legacy for me to cherish and wonderful memories. Momma departed this life October 30, 1985 after a short illness. I miss her dearly and I thank Almighty God for my mother.

Chapter 2

PAST AND PRESENT

*M*y family has always played an important role in my life. They are my champions and I love them dearly. I remember growing up with my siblings in rural Attala County and life was quite adventurous.

Dorothy "Dot" Veasley McMillon is my oldest sister. A lot of responsibility came with being the first born. She had to master her cooking, and housekeeping skills, while working in the fields plowing corn, chopping and picking cotton. She also had to help care for the younger children.

Education was secondary. When it rained too much to work in the fields, she (Sari and James too) was privileged to go to school. She walked about five miles one way to the wood framed New Garden School. It was located across from New Garden Missionary Baptist Church, Kosciusko, Mississippi.

I recall one Saturday that we were walking to town to run errands for Momma. As we walked through a White neighborhood, two teenagers were digging a hole in the front yard. As we passed by them they began throwing dirt in our direction while laughing, but the dirt missed us. We heard the boys say they were going to "sic" (send) their dog on us, and could hear the dog yelping while it was still in the yard. Dot said to me, "Lillie, you better not run. Keep walking, but you better not run. I am going to take care of this."

I must have been around ten or eleven years old at that time. I feared the dog was going to bite me, but I was even more afraid of Dot's wrath if I disobeyed her, and ran from the dog. As the barking dog got closer I still wanted to run. At that time Dot changed the position in which we were walking, and I was on the outer side. This positioned her closest to the yard area as the small dog ran beside and then behind us.

Soon the dog was close to Dot's heel. Without any warning, Dot turned around slightly, raised her foot, and stomped the dog. The dog began yelping loudly as Dot's wrath was being unleashed on him. The mischievous boys yelled, "Lady, he was not going to bother you!" Dot responded sarcastically, "I know!" and we kept walking. I even held my head up high as though running was never on my mind. From that time forth, whenever we walked down that same street we had no further problems.

Dorothy has six children, James (deceased), Otis, Dorothy, Catherine, Sharon, and Trent Veasley.

James Fair ("Tightman," L. C.) is my big brother with his own unique style of poetry. He left home when I was about six years old (c1958), and found a "good job" picking beans, and fruit in the Florida orchards. Before relocating, James had become well aquatinted with hard work in the fields plowing corn, chopping and picking cotton too, as well as acquiring great cooking skills.

Two things stand out most in my mind about him: First, a lovely butterfly flew by one day as we were in the yard. James caught the butterfly and said to me, "If you want a new skirt, bite this butterfly's head off and you will get one just like it." I did not know he was "just being a boy" so yes; I bit off its head! Only a few weeks had passed and one day Momma gave me a new skirt. It was a hand sewn skirt made from the cotton ten pounds sacks that flour was packaged in, back in the day. It was as beautiful as the butterfly. I took my first grade school day picture in that skirt, and still cherish the picture.

Second, before leaving Mississippi for Florida, my big brother found a house for Momma to rent for fifteen dollars a month. At that time, fifteen dollars was a lot of money for a struggling single parent. He encouraged, and finally convinced Momma that she could survive outside of share-cropping. Thank you, big brother, for caring so much about us.

"Tightman" is also a popular mechanic who had his own business in Virginia. He earned the nickname,

"Tightman," because of his excellent skills in repairing means of transportation. The people in his community wanted to call him "Handyman" but someone else had that nickname, therefore, he was called "Tightman." It was a well-known fact among his customers that when "Tightman" completed repairing a vehicle it was going to be right and "tight." We had a wonderful family reunion in October 2012 at his home. "Tightman" is married to Jane (Foeman), and their children are Bryant and Shannel Fair. "Tightman" also has two other children, James Nathan "Whimpy" and Lisa Fair.

Sari Thompson Dodd was born and raised in the country but moved to the city (New Brunswick, New Jersey) with her husband, Lamar Dodd, and children. She too had to master cooking, and housekeeping skills at an early age because it was a matter of survival. Helping with the care of the younger children, and working in the fields was also normal for her. Among family, Sari is famous for her delicious peach cobbler which I am still trying to duplicate.

Sari assisted me when I was old enough to get a summer job. She took me to search for jobs; then she showed me how and where to catch the bus. No matter how tough things were she always had room in her apartment for me.

Sari is blessed to be the mother of ten children, Mary, Dennis, and Milton Thompson, Patricia, Alice, Robert, Cynthia, Barbara, Vicki and Gregory Dodd.

Mary and Annie Ruth were known as those "London girls" in school. I never had to worry about other children bullying me, because they knew not to mess with those London girls' sister.

Mary London Young was the popular one with a walk that would rock the runway. She was mindful of her grades in school and did well. When we all had the mumps, Mary chose to suffer rather than to "rub down in sardine oil" (an old home remedy that was supposed to bring relief).

I recall one day when we came home from school and Momma had supper already cooked. On the stove was a plate of savory-looking pork chops, browned just right, waiting to be consumed. I was so excited because I could tell there was enough for me to get more than one piece. As I gazed at the food, Mary said, "I am not eating that meat. I do not believe it is pork chops, I bet it is deer, and I am not eating Bambi." Annie Ruth and I tried to convince her that was not the case, but Mary was not going to let anyone change her mind.

I proceeded to ask Momma if we could eat supper, and how many pieces of meat could I get. She responded, "As many as you want." Mary then said, "I told you that meat is not pork chops, because we never get as much meat as we want." When I asked Momma what type of meat she had cooked, she replied, "Meat." At that point I did not care if it was deer or not. One thing I did know for sure was that whatever Momma cooked was going to be good. Years later Mary developed a taste for deer and will eat it in moderation.

Mary still watches out for me and I am grateful. She is married to J. C. Young, and they have nine children, Joe Curtis (deceased), Shelia, Jackie, Kevin, Marilyn, LaKesha, Jarvis, Annie, and Isaiah Young.

Annie "Ruth" London Simmons was a real "Tom boy" growing up with a "take charge" kind of spirit. She made good grades but excelled in mathematics. Not only was she conscious about her grades in school, but she even tried to help me cheat in our junior high mathematics class. This was an effort to keep me from failing the class. She finally came to the conclusion that I could not even copy right and stopped trying to help me do so.

When Ruth received Jesus as Lord, she was still bossy but humble. She was concerned about my well-being and gave me tips on how to take care of my vehicles. Ruth served as Head Usher for many years at Faith Temple, and whatever she could do to help this ministry she did it as unto the Lord. Her life came to a close February 2, 2006, in a tragic car accident on her way to work at Tyson's in Carthage.

About six months before her death, the Spirit of God whispered to me one day, "Every time you get a chance, be a blessing to your sister." From that time forth, each time I would do something for Ruth, she would be in the process of doing something for me as well. It seemed both of us were trying to compete with the other in doing good deeds. I finally said, "Look, God told me to be a blessing to you, so stop trying to get ahead of me." We laughed and I had no idea that six months later she would be taken from us all. I thank God for all the precious memories I have of her. Ruth was the mother of two children, Chandra and Reginald Simmons. Her husband, Lee Edward Simmons, preceded her in death in 1979.

Alvin Veasley is my younger brother, and the "left handed genius." That is what the plaque said that hang on his bedroom door when we were teenagers. You did not go in his room for nothing unless you were sent by him. Alvin was unique with his own fashion style. He helped me start my own home business by paying me good when it was his turn to wash dishes.

Out of all the things Alvin paid me for doing, ironing was not one of them. The crease had to be just right. The amount of starch used just right. Somehow, I just could not get it "just right" enough for him. Currently he still irons his own clothes.

Alvin has gained so much wisdom and knowledge over the years and does not mind sharing it with others. It has been gratifying watching him mature over the years. He is married to Jean (Lewis), and their children are, Alvin L. (Chuck) II, Darrell, Larry, and Dushamus. Alvin also has two other children, Alvin D. "Stone" Brown and Glenda Young.

Robert London is the youngest of the family. Momma would be so proud to see how he really takes care of his sisters and extended family members. Robert is a "behind the curtain, I can play the background" kind of man. He prefers that his deeds are done to the glory and honor of God, and if recognition is to be given, give it to someone else. He is an intelligent and humble man, who retired from the United States Army.

Robert is also very humorous, and he displayed his humor at our 2012 family reunion. I find him to be prophetic as well. Alvin was all dressed up looking real dignified, and Robert volunteered him to close with prayer on that Friday night. Robert stated, "We are helping to usher him into his calling." I stand with you on that prophesy little brother. Robert is married to Evangelist Alean (Brown) London.

Mary Ann Thompson Simmons is my niece (Sari's daughter), reared by Momma, so she is more like a sister. For Mary's seventh grade Transition Program I had promised to purchase her a pair of white shoes. The shoes she chose had a small buckle on it and cost only fifty cents more than a pair I preferred. Because I termed the shoes "worldly," she had to settle for the pair I had chosen. Actually there was nothing wrong with the shoes she wanted. I later apologized and learned to be a bit more practical. Sometimes we can get so heavenly minded that we are of little earthly good.

Years later the Lord began to draw Mary close to Him and she surrendered her life to Jesus! Even now, we still act like sisters! We especially love shopping together, visiting other churches, and cruising on the high seas. She and her husband, W.C. Simmons, are the parents of six children, W.C. Jr. and Christopher (deceased), Laurie, Camille, Marie, and Kegan Simmons.

Family is very important to me and I thank God for the family he blessed me to be a part of. Each one is unique, but all of us have a good dosage of Momma in us and that is a good thing!

CHAPTER 3

MR. DEAN

1966-1968

*I*n the educational arena, I had wonderful teachers. The former Northside Elementary, Tipton Street High, and Long Creek High Schools, afforded me access to quality learning. Yet, among my many teachers there was one who was in a category all by himself. That teacher was "Mr. Dean."

Long before Saxon Math, and state tests such as Mississippi State Assessment Test, and the Common Core state standards, there was Mr. William K. Dean. He was one of those instructors you heard about in junior high, and prayed that he would retire before your time to take his class in high school.

Mr. Dean was a clean shaven man, neatly dressed with his shirt tucked in his trousers, accented with a belt, and nice shoes. He always stood at the door to greet his students as they arrived for class. Not even the bold or beautiful wanted to be late for his class. Mr. Dean did not play and he was very passionate about mathematics. I believe he felt he was obligated to instill that same passion, and love he had for mathematics into the minds of the students he taught.

Mr. Dean not only had a reputation for being a serious teacher but he also displayed a genuine love for his students. I recall Mr. Dean taking the time to counsel me one day. His overall attitude toward me seemed to emphasize that "Failure was not an option." It appeared he had a passion for everything! What I didn't know till years later was that Mr. Dean was a born again Christian, who valued his relationship with the Lord. That set him apart as a young African American male instructor and he was not ashamed to be different.

In high school I was a below average student with grades ranging from high D's to middle C's, and I thought that was just fine. I had Mr. Dean as mathematics instructor in the 9th and 10th grade, and my goal was to at least "C" my way out of his class. My good elementary grades did not follow me as I no longer applied myself.

Then Mr. Dean began his counsel. When he talked it was hard not to listen. "Lillie, you can do better than what you are doing in my class. You and your little friends can do better. You are hanging with the wrong crowd (referring to some of my buddies), and you need to do something about your grades in my class. I believe you can do the work."

Mr. Dean acted as if he knew there were times my friends and I would plan not to do our homework. I even wondered if he overheard our conversations in the hallway as we exchanged classes. It was during that time we sometimes agreed not to do the homework he assigned.

My best friend at Tipton Street High, Arnita Woodard, maintained good grades, even though she sometimes partnered with me in skipping homework. Somehow, I just could not manage my grades as she did, but after that counseling session with Mr. Dean I vowed to improve. I became more focused and by the end of the 11th grade I was an overall B-C student.

In the fall of 1969, my senior year, I transferred to Long Creek High School as Momma had a house built in the Sallis area. My grades continued to improve, and I was an A-B student, with A's dominating my report card! My best friend at Long Creek High, Lillie Diane Bentley, was a high achiever and my neighbor, so I really had to stay focused. My self-esteem was much higher now because I was realizing my potential to excel.

I attained an ACT score of fifteen, and had the highest grade average for the first semester. Still, because of my overall high school grade average, I ranked only number 13 out of 44 students in the graduating class of 1970. My lack of dedication early on in high school reared its ugly head, and finally caught up with me, but I never forgot Mr. Dean.

I am grateful for the way he influenced my life. His overall concern made me rethink my options, and I chose to reach for excellence.

Today "Mr. Dean" is Superintendent William K. Dean, an Elder, and Pastor of St. Paul Church of God in Christ, in Lexington, Mississippi. "Mr. Dean" is still watching out for the welfare of children, the souls of mankind and definitely a part of "a village."

I believe that all pupils need to know they are of value and "greatness lies within each student." That was the message

"Mr. Dean" was trying so hard to convey to me. He had confidence in me when I did not fully value my own capability. "Mr. Dean" laid a good foundation for me by being a positive role model, strategically placed by God to bring change in my life, naturally and spiritually.

Chapter 4

EVENTS ON MY JOURNEY TO NEW JERSEY

It was late May 1969, and school was finally out for the summer. Thoughts of traveling by bus to New Brunswick, New Jersey, in June dominated my thoughts. After all, for this sixteen year old up-coming senior, any summer spent way from my small town of Kosciusko, Mississippi, was exciting!

Somehow, I just knew the summer job my sister, Sari, told me about would aid in spicing up my wardrobe for school in the fall. I visualized the stares I would get from the girls as I walked down the halls in my "city-looking clothes." It would be like the fashions of the east were prancing around in the south. Absolutely wonderful, I thought!

The Wednesday of my departure soon arrived. The big Trailways bus pulled up to the local bus station around nine o'clock in the morning, and Momma bid me farewell. Of course, there were the last minute reminders to behave myself, and not give my sister any trouble. "Bye Momma," I said, with the usual teary eyes. This was my second trip to Jersey, and I always cried when leaving Mom. Then I would cry when leaving Sara to return back to Mississippi.

Traveling by bus was tiring and enjoyable at the same time. Still, I was anxious to arrive in New Brunswick, mingle with my relatives, and see what kinds of jobs were available for me to check out. Every time I took a nap and awakened, I was getting closer to my destination.

I had checked my ticket several times, but glanced at it again as the bus was within the suburbs of Philadelphia, Pennsylvania. According to my ticket, I had an hour layover in Philadelphia. However, as the bus pulled into the Philadelphia station around nine thirty that Thursday night, I noticed people carrying signs saying "ON STRIKE."

Like everyone else, I approached the ticket counter and inquired about my connecting bus. The agent spoke as if reading from a prepared statement. I was informed "No buses are leaving the city tonight. The station will close at eleven o'clock, and no one can spend the night inside. If you like, hotel accommodations can be made at your own expense."

This information shocked me! I wished I had known the bus drivers were on strike before I left home, because I could have waited till later to travel. Now my sister was at work and would be expecting me to arrive in New Brunswick at the scheduled time. Even worse, I did not have the extra money for hotel accommodations.

I had learned in my social studies class that Philadelphia was known as the "City of Brotherly Love," but where was the extra compassion I needed? This once confident sixteen year old was about to fall to pieces. Seeing the distraught look on my face, the ticket agent informed me that local buses would honor my ticket. She pointed me in the right direction and wished me well.

I picked up my small carry-on suitcase, walked past the angry-looking strikers, and headed for the local bus stop about one half block from the Trailways bus station. I finally reached the area, and casually surveyed my surroundings. If my mind was not playing tricks on me, from the crowd of people it appeared a West Indies man was staring at me. I dismissed the uneasiness temporarily because at least I was surrounded by other people.

Soon a local bus arrived, and I gave him my ticket. The driver rudely stated, "This bus ain't going to Trenton, New Jersey." Then he added, "The bus you want should be arriving shortly." Without exchanging words, I stepped off the bus disappointed, regained my composure and moved back onto the sidewalk.

About fifteen minutes later another bus pulled up to the bus stop, and I gave him my ticket. The driver said, "I cannot take that ticket, only tokens or coins." I asked, "Why?" and informed the driver that the Trailways Company said my ticket would be honored by the local buses. The driver simply said, "Lady, I'm sorry, but this bus only takes tokens or coins." Well, I got off the bus visibly frustrated. By now I'm wondering if I will ever get out of what appeared to be a God-forsaken city, not a city of brotherly love.

Then the West Indies man stepped forward, and introduced himself as "Porjoa." "Lady," he said, "I've been watching you, and in case you do not know by now, no bus is going to

Trenton tonight. Perhaps I can help you, but we will have to talk to my girlfriend, Minnie, who is at work now. She works nearby and gets off at midnight."

I thought, girl what are you about to do? You do not know this man! After all, wait a minute! Your girlfriend is at work and you are not. You are sitting around watching people, and you want me to do what? I may not look like a city girl, but give me credit for a little common sense! My mind was running wild.

I finally said, "Thanks, but I think the next bus will be the right one." The man returned to his former position of sitting on the little ledge protruding from the nearby building, and I stood waiting for the next bus.

Shortly, a young Caucasian male walked up and said, "So you are headed to Jersey, so am I. Just follow me and I will make sure you get on the right bus. The next one should be coming in just a few minutes, and it is the last bus for the night." With a sigh of relief I said "thanks."

The bus arrived around eleven forty five, and people began boarding. The young man beckoned for me to follow him. He dropped his coins into the machine, got a ticket and sat down. He then motioned that he was saving a seat for me. The driver accepted my ticket but still I asked, "Are you going to Trenton tonight?" "Yes," he replied, "But are you sure you want to go tonight?" "Sure," I said, "Why do you ask?" The driver responded, "The bus station closed at eleven o'clock tonight and will not reopen until five o'clock Friday morning. You will be standing on the outside for several hours. I can drop you off but that is all I can do."

At that point I looked directly into the face of the young Caucasian man. He looked as if he had just gotten caught with his hand in the cookie jar. I was sixteen years old but I quickly decided that traveling to Trenton would not be in my best interest.

After retrieving my ticket, I stepped off the bus disappointed again. Thoughts of never seeing my Mom or my sister flashed through my mind. The summer job, new school clothes, and possible jealous girls at school were not important anymore. I had no way to contact my sister. How in the world would I, a country girl from the south, survive a night on the streets of this big city? What about that man still sitting on the ledge of the building?

Porjoa approached me again and said, "It is about time for my girlfriend to get off work. I will not bother you. As a matter of fact, you do not have anything I want, so just relax." With no other alternative I agreed to go with him. We walked to Minnie's job and discussed my dilemma.

Next, we went to a pay phone to call Momma. While speaking with the telephone operator I made the perfect collect call home. When Momma said "Hello" I started crying uncontrollably. Minnie immediately took the phone, and started trying to explain to Momma what was going on. Now both Momma and I are crying. Can you imagine what my mother must have been thinking at that time? Later, after I settled down, Minnie returned the phone back to me.

Momma agreed for me to spend the night with the strangers as I had nowhere else to go. We cried over the phone, exchanged what we thought was a final "I love you," and said good-bye.

Upon reaching Porjoa and Minnie's apartment, I was made welcome to share their sleeping accommodations-a mattress on the floor. Porjoa assured me no harm would come to me as he would sleep next to the wall, Minnie in the middle, and I on the outer side. All of us slept ready-to-roll (fully dressed) that night.

The next morning I awakened "alive" and was grateful to God and the strangers. For breakfast we ate a simple meal of leftover greens (spinach or turnips) and corn bread. This was an unusual breakfast for me; however, I ate the food, was grateful and silently humbled. They had so little but were willing to share even that.

We took our showers and got dressed early that Friday morning. We returned to the Trailways bus station and conversed with an agent handling grievances regarding the bus strike. Porjoa wanted them to issue me a ticket for the local buses so I would not encounter any more problems, but the agent still affirmed that my Trailways ticket was fine.

Porjoa told Minnie and I to go to the waiting room while he talked to the agent alone. Minnie gave me that "It may get ugly in there" look as we started down the hallway. When Porjoa returned, he had a big smile on his face as he waved the local bus ticket in his hand that would take me to New Brunswick, via New York City, New York.

While waiting for the bus to arrive I asked if we could take some pictures. By the time I pulled out my Polaroid instamatic camera Porjoa said I could not take pictures of them. Somehow Minnie convinced him that it would cause no harm for me to have one picture. By the time I took their picture, and Minnie took a few of me for them, my local bus was within view. I asked for their address so we could keep in touch, and Porjoa refused. He said they planned to relocate to New York City within a few weeks so I gave them my sister's address in New Jersey. They promised to visit me as they traveled to New York City but never did. Regretfully, I have never seen or heard from my "God-sent rescuers" again, but I cherished the picture.

I am finally on the bus destined for New York City. The ride seemed short, and after my arrival I obtained my small carry on suitcase, and proceeded to my next departure gate. While walking, a nicely dressed African American young man approached me. He asked if I needed help with my luggage.

Here we go again, I thought. This is New York City, known for muggers, and crazy happenings, and you want to help me with what? "No thanks, I am fine," I said. "Look lady," he replied, "I am only here to help you. I can tell you are not from here by the way you carry your purse. Now let me have the luggage, put your shoulder bag strap over your head, and hang on to your purse. I will escort you where you need to go. No strings attached. Okay?" "Alright," I said, and as we stood face to face I saw he was wearing a unique kind of hat, but somehow I felt safe with him.

When we reached my departure gate, he wished me well and tipped his hat. I thanked him for his assistance and he went back in the same direction we had come. I have never seen my God sent protector again. So yes, I boarded that bus to New Jersey with a smile. When I arrived in New Brunswick, my sister met me with hugs and tears of joy. Her face had that look of relief, for her little sister had finally made it safely after a three day ordeal. "I am so glad to see you girl. You are the best thing I have seen all day," she said.

My journey to New Jersey had been filled with unforgettable events, and I was so grateful the drama had finally ended. On that Sunday evening as we watched the news, I was quite surprised at what I saw. The news showed a clipping of a group known as the Green Beret volunteers. They were patrolling bus and train stations in New York City in an effort to curtail crime.

The volunteers made headline news for acts of heroism in the face of danger, and wore the same unique kind of hat as my former rescuer. I shouted excitedly to my sister who was in the kitchen, "He was a Green Beret volunteer, that young man who carried my luggage at the bus station. He really was there to protect me like he said!"

On the following Monday I began my search for a summer job as planned. All the drama was behind me and I could move forward with life. I had no idea that there was still more drama to come.

I placed applications with the businesses my sister recommended, and was becoming more familiar with the city. A few days after my arrival to New Brunswick, I was waiting for the bus that would transport me to my next promising interview. A friendly young man whom I had seen a few times at the bus stop approached me, and we began to talk. We had conversed before so I did not consider him a total stranger.

The sky had become cloudy as if rain could be in the forecast. The young man capitalized on the weather, and stated that I really needed an umbrella since "sugar melts in the rain." I knew he was flirting but so what. No harm done and "no red flags" of impending danger popped up in my mind.

He stated he lived upstairs in the next building and would get me an umbrella as it appeared the bus was running late. A few minutes later, he reappeared at the entrance of the doorway, and asked if I would help him locate the umbrella as he was having difficulty finding it. Still, "no red flags" darted in my mind.

I proceeded to climb the staircase and entered the economy style apartment. Upon entering, the door was slammed closed, and I was thrown on the bed nearby. His economy apartment consisted of two rooms, bedroom combined with kitchenette, and a bathroom. Now the struggle was on! I was fighting for my life as I realized rape was the underlying motive all along.

The country girl from the south was not working out very well at all. How would my sister ever find me if things did not work out in my favor? Would I ever see Momma or my family again? After all, I was supposed to be at the bus stop going for an interview. Common sense told me that I was going to lose that battle. Yes, many thoughts were bombarding my mind as I attempted to struggle from the grips of my attacker.

The once friendly young man had transformed into a living nightmare. I realized he was much stronger than I and hope of leaving that apartment unharmed began to fade. Then I heard a voice say, "play dead." In the midst of the commotion I thought, "play dead," that does not make much sense as I will probably end up dead anyhow. The voice spoke again, "play dead." Not knowing who the voice belonged to, I decided to obey. I stopped struggling immediately, and just lay on the bed lifeless. The man noticed the change and stopped the attack. He started slapping my face and asking me if I was alright, but I did not move a muscle.

I felt him release me and then he got off the bed. I could hear water running in the bathroom, yet I remained very still. He returned, and began washing my face with an extremely wet towel in an attempt to revive me. I could hear him saying, "I'm so sorry, I'm so sorry, are you alright?"

I lay motionless for a few more minutes in an effort to convince him he should not resume the attack. Then I began to "awaken" slowly, while asking, "Where am I?" The man replied, "I am so sorry for what I was trying to do, I did not know you were a virgin (And yes, I just played innocent because I needed to get out of that apartment alive). I am going to take real good care of you, and when you turn eighteen, we'll talk about going further. I'll be at the bus stop every morning to make sure no one bothers you," he said. After I regained my composure, he escorted me back to the bus stop as if I was his new girlfriend.

Yes, I returned in time to catch the bus, made it to the interview, and was hired as a nurse's aide for the summer. I never saw my attacker again, because at least I was smart enough to catch the bus from another location.

During that time, I was not a born again Christian, but I believe the Lord extended His grace and mercy unto me. He preserved my life for a reason. Those experiences changed my outlook on life. I developed a greater appreciation for simple things like "life, family, and daily food." I discovered that not all strangers are immoral; share what you have with others, even if you only have a little. I learned that sometimes you cannot repay the person who came to your rescue, but **you can certainly help someone else on life's journey. So go out of your way to be kind to someone else! Join the R.A.K Club** (Random Acts of Kindness). Fulfill Matthew 23:36-40 . . . Thou shalt love thy neighbor as thyself . . .

Yes, Philadelphia, Pennsylvania, indeed lived up to its reputation as the "City of Brotherly Love." New York City, the "city that never sleeps," let us continue to make this world a better place in as many ways as we can. God bless you Philly and New York City.

ADVANCING TOWARD
REDEMPTION FROM SIN

Some teenagers of today seem to be spiraling downward, and making poor choices with little regard to the consequences that follow. Priorities are all mixed up, and not enough emphasis is placed on things pertaining to spirituality.

As for me, I was an average fun-loving teen, with a special interest in the fashions of the day. Yes, at eighteen years of age, my life still revolved around worldly things. It was May 1971, and life as I had once known it would never be the same. In an hour or so the sun would be setting. Shades of orange and yellow had already begun to cast its reflections in the background as the sun proceeded to bid "good day."

I entered the front door of our rural home nestled among the tall gum trees, surrounded by big tin tubs of Momma's prized Water Lilies. Soon, a sparkling white two-door, 1965 Thunderbird pulled into the driveway. It was a real cool looking car that easily got your attention. To my surprise, a young man stepped out wearing black slacks, and a baby blue long sleeve shirt. His hair was cut short,

and the smile on his brown-sugar face revealed a brilliant sparkle in his eyes that seemed to dance. "Hi Lillie," he said, "It's me, James, James Miller."

It had been over a year since I had seen this once "love of my life." From his outward appearance I could tell that he had grown into quite a young man at twenty years of age. The "player look" (ladies' man) was gone, as if maturity and responsibility had finally caught up, and overtaken him. This new look was quite different from his usual street clothes of fashionable dark pants, and partially unbuttoned shirt. I presumed he had come in search of me and thought that was real sweet of him.

I invited him in and informed Momma of his arrival. He sat down on the cozy sectional sofa, and I proceeded to sit next to him. Immediately, he moved away from me as if something or someone had prompted him to do so. Now that really got my attention. I could not imagine the James I once knew rejecting an advance from me. After all, we had dated periodically since he was fifteen and I was thirteen. "Is something wrong?" I asked. "No," he replied, "It is just that I have changed. I am not the same James you used to know. I have given my life to Jesus and have gotten saved. I am sanctified now, and I do not even have a girlfriend. I am interested in what pleases the Lord, and do not accommodate my flesh anymore."

Clearly stunned, I just looked at him. In one month I would be nineteen years old, and I had been a "church girl" for as long as I could remember. Yet what did he mean when he put so much emphasis on "being saved?" Oh well, I will just have to figure it out later I told myself.

Like James, I too had physically changed. No longer was I the tall, short-haired, skinny, and the almost shy girl he once dated. My physical features were more defined now, and I had no problem attracting the attention of the opposite sex. Going to church was normal for me, and I did not see where having a boyfriend would interfere with that.

"I came to invite you to Bible study tonight," James said. "Tonight," I said, as if a formal request in advance would be more appropriate. Still, without taking his pleading eyes off me, and gesturing with his hands, he said, "yes, tonight. I can wait until you get dressed."

Meanwhile, as I pondered for an answer to his invitation, he began to tell me about his church and pastor. He informed me that the Bible study would be held in the pastor's home and that people would be praying, singing, and sometimes shouting. The pastor was Evangelist Lillie B. Sanlin, but was called "Sister Sanlin." He said she had really helped him to see the light.

Reluctantly, I agreed to attend the Bible study in an effort to please him. Guess what though? I had my own mental agenda regarding us, and convinced myself that this was only a phase James was going through.

I took my time getting dressed, and chose a conservative looking beige linen mini-dress with matching pastel flowered jacket. Shortly thereafter, we left for service and my sister, Mary, also came. The twelve-mile drive back to town seemed long, but James continued to talk about his pastor and church family.

Finally we arrived at the pastor's residence, 310 East Street, a white wood framed home with nice lawn. James opened the screen door that led into a well-kept living room. Straight chairs had been brought in to accommodate the expected over flow of attendees.

Standing in the doorway leading into the kitchen stood a tall, confident looking woman. James introduced us and she extended a warm welcome, and thanked me for coming. In the meantime, I sat down next to one of the ladies, but my thoughts began to wander. So this was the renowned evangelist James referred to as "Sister Sanlin." This was the single woman without a job, who walked by faith, and depended on God to meet her needs.

Singing interrupted my thoughts signaling service was starting. After prayer, scripture reading, and testimony service, Sister Sanlin began to minister. The people opened their Bible to the passage she was teaching from. Since I did not have a Bible with me, the lady near me positioned her Bible so I could read along. The scripture was Proverbs 14:34, Righteousness exalteth a nation but sin is a reproach to any people.

When the entire Bible study ended the call to discipleship was made (altar call). I realized that I did not have the experience of salvation that Sister Sanlin, and James had referred to as being "saved." I had not truly repented of my sins (been sorry to God for sins committed), and received Jesus as Lord and Savior. Sometimes I had actually been sorry, sorry I got caught in a lie or something, but not really sorry toward God.

I had even prayed sometimes. Prayed that God would get me out of the mess I had gotten myself in, and I promised Him I would not do it again. Well, that promise was short-lived.

Though I did not make a commitment that night, I felt something happening within me that I could not explain. As we said good night, and approached the screen door, Sister Sanlin called me aside. She whispered, "Young ladies who care about, and respect themselves (referring to my mini dress and exposed thighs), cover their bodies appropriately." I smiled and said, "Thank you." My mother was firm on respect so I knew how to respond. We made our way to the car, conversed casually and James dropped us off at home.

The following Monday night James returned to the house. He informed me it was Youth Service night, and somehow he thought I had accepted his invitation for service at Sister Sanlin's. In the meantime, I thought he came because we had discussed him taking me to Long Creek Elementary School in Sallis, Mississippi.

"What? I don't remember having a conversation like that," I responded, "No way! This was my very special niece's (Mary) 7th to 8th grade Transition Program, and I was not about to miss that occasion. Why we were like sisters! How could I not go?" As a matter of fact, I thought it was understood that we would go together. Now I had no other way to get there since Momma had already left for the program.

Someway, somehow, James convinced me to attend the Youth Service. The fellowship was wonderful, but I was still trying to figure out why I had chosen church over my niece's program. After all, I had only planned to visit at Sister Sanlin's periodically, if at all and this was just too soon. Like I said, I had my own agenda.

Let me back up a minute. My first encounter with "Sister Sanlin" was at a Thursday night Bible class held in her home. As I prepared for work the following day (Friday) I had a tough time selecting what to wear. Finally, I settled for a plaid dress that came to the top of my knees. A new found peace overcame me as I went to work, and later to town. While shopping in town the first person I met on the street was, guess who? "Sister Sanlin." Somehow I did not feel inappropriately dressed. I felt like a lady. Her statement about dressing was implanted in my spirit. Why, my own mother had been trying for years to convince me that my manner of dressing was inappropriate, and I just did not get it.

Little did I know that the Lord had begun the sanctifying process in my life. You see, relatives had already informed me that most people who visited "Sister Sanlin's" home ministry were never the same. To my family, neighbors, and even myself, after that first Bible study, I too, was never the same. One aunt wanted to know what I needed to get saved from. According to her, I was a good church girl,

intelligent and respectful. I was alright like I was she said. When Momma shared that conversation with me I responded, "If she only knew about the real Lillie!"

Now back to Church. While in the Youth Service that Monday night, the Spirit of the Lord began to convict my heart and I did make a commitment to Jesus, though not openly. The Lord continued to bring conviction in my heart and about a week later I was baptized in Jesus' name according to Acts 2:38 (Repent, and be baptized, every one of you, in the name of Jesus for the remission of sins, and ye shall receive the power of the Holy Ghost.). I pursued after and received the baptism of the Holy Ghost. Yes, I was beginning to understand what being "saved" was all about! I no longer had an underlying agenda. This was not a phase but a life style. Thereafter, James and I had a simple brother and sister relationship. Of course, I was grateful to James for the day he came "in search of me" that I might have the opportunity to truly gain Christ. I had begun to sell out to Jesus and obey the word of God in Matthew 6:33, "Seek ye first the kingdom of God and his righteousness . . ."

I thank God for His grace and mercy that he extends to all mankind. He desires that all individuals would be saved, delivered from the bondage of sin, and inherits eternal life. When you receive Jesus as Savior, you choose life; reject Him and you choose damnation (destruction, separation from God in the lake of fire and brimstone). O taste and see that the Lord is good: blessed is the man that trusteth in him. (Psalms 34:8)

Chapter 6

LILLIE B. SANLIN

(SWEETIE, SISTER SANLIN, PASTOR SANLIN, MOM)

The late James and Annie Jackson Sanlin welcomed the arrival of their third daughter, born April 28, 1925, given the name of Lillie Bell. She was known to friends and relatives simply as "Sweetie." Before she was born, Mrs. Sanlin prayed the following prayer: "Lord whatever this child be, boy or girl, I give it back to you." How many mothers today are willing to sincerely dedicate their unborn child to the Lord, for Him to use as He chooses? Thank God, this mother did. Many have witnessed the anointing of God resting heavily upon that child, and the ministry God later assigned to her hand.

Of course, she was a normal child growing up, doing normal everyday things. There was a time when you could find her around the house with her foot on top of a watermelon rind. Nothing uncommon about that, except this particular rind held a cat captive underneath. Her mother finally heard the muffled cries of the distressed cat, and came to its rescue. She also brought a switch for the mischievous little girl.

At the age of five she "set off to discover that little white house, with the white refrigerator and stove she often dreamed about." Fortunately for her, she returned back in time for supper. She did find that particular house in 1969 when she lived at 310 East Street, Kosciusko, Mississippi.

She attended the Antioch Public School, Concorda Public School and Greenville Industrial College (Greenville, Mississippi). She taught school for one year at the Concorda Public School, Concorda, Mississippi.

She was saved in 1954 in the Church of God in Christ. It was her first trip to the altar when she received the power of the Holy Ghost. After considerable growth in the Lord, she was led to minister to the sick and shut-in. While living in Memphis, Tennessee, she carried fruit baskets to many in the hospital. She also carried hand-made dolls to the children in the hospital who had no parents.

Even though she had been filled with the power of the Holy Ghost, she was baptized in Jesus' name at the Bethlehem Healing Temple, Chicago, Illinois. In 1967, her full understanding, and knowledge of the baptism in Jesus' name was completely opened up by the Lord.

I had the opportunity to meet Pastor Sanlin in 1971 when she was referred to as "Sister Sanlin" by most people. Later, those close to her, even Bishops, called her "Mom" with the utmost respect.

Yes, there was something about Sister Sanlin's demeanor that warranted reverence. She appeared to be about forty five years of age. Her hair was shoulder length, black, delicately streaked with silver strands, and many stylish curls combed away from her forehead. The curls would fall to the side of her face, accenting her big brown eyes that seemed to penetrate deep into the soul. Her light brown facial complexion was make-up free, yet her face seemed to glow with joy. The smile on her face was broad and appeared genuine. She walked in sheer confidence, articulated well, and used her hands to aid in verbalizing.

Sister Sanlin's wardrobe for ministry consisted mostly of robes, black, and white dresses that came well below the calves of her legs. She took extra precaution to make sure the neckline of her clothing was high enough with no exposure of cleavage. The sleeves on her garments were long or three quarters in length. Her clothing was not transparent or tight-fitting. This overall image was what I later labeled as "That Black Pentecostal Look." I soon discovered that I would respect this "look" as well.

She used time wisely, enjoyed teaching about obedience to God's word, and compliance to the laws of the land. Gathering around the kitchen table created an atmosphere to discuss matters deemed important. She often stated that God holds us responsible for gaining wholesome knowledge, and then applying it to our daily lives.

The Lord anointed Sister Sanlin as a vocalist as well. In c1972-1973, she recorded four songs on a 45 RPM album, with L. Hess serving as musician (piano and organ). God's anointing was evident as she sang "Walk with me Lord," "Just a Closer Walk with Thee," "I Found the Answer" and "Blessed Assurance."

However, she was not always anointed to sing. Sister Sanlin shared this story with me: As a young girl, she always desired to sing, and would volunteer to do so on several youth programs at her church. Yet, she stated, her singing was so bad, till her mother threatened to whip her if she continued to attempt singing publicly.

On this particular occasion she wanted to sing so badly. She knew what the consequence could be, but decided to take a chance anyway, avoiding "That you're going to get it look!" from her mother. Upon reaching the platform, she opened her mouth to sing, and "beautiful music" came forth. Her mother and the entire church were surprised, and so was she. God had granted the desire of her heart. Thereafter, she sang joyfully to the glory of God.

Sister Sanlin later became my "second mother" and mentor. Her manner of approach made me eager to hear what she had to say, and give it serious deliberation.

She had a wonderful sense of humor. Whenever I did something she did not approve of, she would pull my nose. This of course brought laughter to those sitting around, until it was their turn for a nose pulling. If she did something outstanding, she would have us give her a pat on the head.

Sister Sanlin was very thorough when it came to housekeeping. She was an excellent cook, and periodically would invite senior citizens over for lunch. She taught the young ladies that when preparing food for others, it is vital that the food look appealing, and should never be placed carelessly on the plate.

Like my mother, Sister Sanlin had confidence in my ability to excel as a secretary. My on-the-job training began when I served as church secretary. I was encouraged by her to pursue excellence in everything I attempted to accomplish. She was an advocate of education, emphasizing that the Lord needed intelligent individuals too.

Values like honesty and perseverance were reinforced. She gave instructions on how to cope with destructive and constructive criticism. "You can use criticism to improve yourself," she would say. Because of her Bible based teaching, preaching, and overall influence, my spiritual life accelerated, as I endeavored to showcase Christianity in every aspect of my living.

*   *   *

AN EXAMPLE OF TRUE HOLINESS
"MOM"

Mom labored tirelessly for the Lord. She loved Him, and wanted people from all walks of life to be healed (physically, spiritually, and emotionally), and set free from the bondage of sin. Her ministry was much like our current church's Mission Statement – "Ministry to the Whole Man."

On one occasion Mom had been invited to be the keynote speaker for a "Women's Day service in Memphis, Tennessee. Her subject was entitled, "Will the Real Women of God Please Stand Up and be Counted?" I must say that the anointing of the Holy Ghost was upon Pastor Sanlin as she ministered the word of God! She preached holiness in regards to envy, strife, jealousy, and how clothing alone does not mean we are saved.

Mothers of the church, and sisters in very sophisticated hats and suits were crying, and some shouting. Deliverance flowed from the pulpit to the ushers at the back door. God showed Himself mighty with signs and wonders.

My friend, the plea is still being heard today. Will the real people of God stand up and be counted? Be counted as one whose lifestyle will not bring shame to the Lord or the church.

In 1974, Pastor Sanlin, being led of the Lord, planned a service called "Jubilee." She commissioned Evangelist Nazarene Brown and me to write an "Occasion." We were given background information and then instructed to start writing. She returned later to see how well we were doing and was pleased. We confessed that it had taken much prayer, concentration, and dependence on the Holy Ghost. It also involved information I was gathering for my book, writing and rewriting, before the finished product emerged. Pastor Sanlin fine-tuned the article, and next you will read the occasion for our first annual Jubilee celebration.

<u>OCCASION</u>

Praise the Lord,

We, the members of the Faith Temple Pentecostal Church Mission, have set aside this day, November 3, 1974, to give special thanks unto our Lord, for His favor He has shown us.

Yet, we shall never be able to say, "Lord I thank you," for all He has done for us. We can say as the psalmist said, "Many, O Lord my God, are thy wonderful works which thou hast done, and thy thoughts which are to us-ward: they cannot be reckoned up in order unto thee: If I would declare and speak of them, they are more than can be numbered." (Psalm 40:5)

The calendar has its various dates of celebration, so why shouldn't we have a special day of thanks unto the Lord? As the wise King Solomon said in Proverbs 15:3, "The eyes of the Lord are in every place, beholding the evil and the good."

Truly the Lord's all-seeing eyes beheld the evil, and the good taking place in Kosciusko, Mississippi. God saw the need for a humble and faithful leader. One that would stand steadfast on his word, with no respect of person. One that would seek His face through much fasting, and unlimited prayer for the souls of man.

As the Lord considered the destiny of many souls in Kosciusko, He spoke to Evangelist Lillie B. Sanlin, (a native of Mississippi) while she was fulfilling a seven month mission work in the state of Texas, 1967. This woman of God did not have Kosciusko on her mind. As we often heard Evangelist Sanlin say, "Only two of us came to this town (1968), Jesus and me." Still, when you know that Jesus is with you there is no need to fear.

As the Lord dealt with the heart of Evangelist Sanlin concerning the work He had prepared for her here, she willingly obeyed the Lord. She arrived in this town, July 3, 1969, from her residence in Zion, Illinois. She came with a willing mind to do her utmost to help men and women, to come out of darkness, into His, (the Lord's) marvelous light.

The church was organized November 18, 1969 with prayer meetings held each Thursday night at her residence. There were a few attending these services but they were faithful followers. The first Sunday school class began the first Sunday in January 1970. This too was held in the home of Evangelist Sanlin for about two years.

In September of 1971, we moved to the Brush Harbor, which was located only a few feet away from this very establishment. After six weeks, due to the change in weather, we moved from there to Brother and Sister R. V. Alston's vacant home in Ethel, Mississippi. Through it all the Lord kept right on blessing. After a short time, God blessed "Sister Sanlin" to build a house for Him, along with the faithful few.

We entered this structure on the 19th of March, 1972. God has fulfilled His word, even as he spoke to Solomon in Second Chronicles 7:12. In the midst of conflicts, discouragement, and evil forces on every hand, this great woman kept the vision. Today we behold this vision which has been fulfilled before our very eyes, after a short period of four years. All along her heart was strengthened by the Lord. In November 1971, the Lord spoke to Evangelist Sanlin and told her, "You have no troubles, for your troubles are my troubles," assuring her that He would fight all her battles.

Our Pastor often recalls the night when the power of the Lord was so great in our midst, until as they came off the street they began to rejoice. A heavy rain was falling on the outside, yet there was a great Holy Ghost rain falling on the inside. This very night three souls were baptized with the Holy Ghost.

On September 20, 1974, Faith Temple Pentecostal Church number two was organized in Decatur, Illinois, under her leadership. In addition, the Faith Temple Christian Academy was founded in 1981.

* * *

From the early days when the Lord first called her, Pastor Sanlin demonstrated tremendous spiritual power as countless miracles had been performed through her. He sent forth this missionary on a path that has led her to various corners of the earth. She traveled doing the Lord's work throughout the southern part of the United States, Canada, Mexico, Rome, The Virgin Islands, and the Holy Land.

The Lord empowered Pastor Sanlin to complete two forty day fasts. She stated that during one of those fasts, she became so hungry. Rather than submit to the temptation and cravings of her body for food, she took canned goods out of the pantry. She sat on her kitchen floor and read the labels (ingredients inside the cans). This gave assurance to her flesh that in due time food would be eaten.

Determination is a key element to accomplishing the task at hand. When God orchestrates or ordains that a thing be accomplished, His Holy Spirit will **"enable"** us to complete the assignment. We get the victory and He gets the glory (honor).

Prior to the construction of the church in 1972, Pastor Sanlin encountered problems securing land and financing for the building. No lending institution wanted to loan money to a female minister. After all, she did not have a job, and there were no male members employed in the church available to sign the loan transaction.

The Lord had a ram in the bush though. Two sisters, Annie Bowie Johnson and Fannie Bowie, donated two acres of land for the church. In spite of criticism, they pressed forth. They were generous in their giving for ministry needs, and testified often of God's goodness. Sister Annie played the guitar skillfully, and is remembered for the songs, "When I see the Blood," and "Yes Lord, keep ringing in my Soul."

The Lord again gave Pastor Sanlin favor, and financing was approved for construction of the church. He had also shown her in a vision the blueprint for the church as well. Although the contractor did not follow all the specifications Pastor Sanlin outlined, the building was complete in March 1972. About 10 ½ years later, special services to celebrate the Mortage Burning (pay off of the loan), Laying of Cornerstone, and Church Dedication were held August 27-29, 1982. The "Faithful Few" had remained faithful to God and the ministry. In turn, the Lord had added to the church many more members as he continued to show Himself mighty.

Many souls were snatched from impending judgment through Pastor Sanlin's ministry. God blessed her with supernatural strength to birth and preside over this organization. I know, for I was there, an eye witness to the awesome power of an awesome God working through a yielded vessel. Someone may say I only "scratched the surface" in regards to her ministry. To you I say, "Write your own book, for her ministry was too vast for one individual to tell it all. I look forward to hearing a continuation of the story." She is gone but definitely not forgotten. These things have been written, lest we forget!

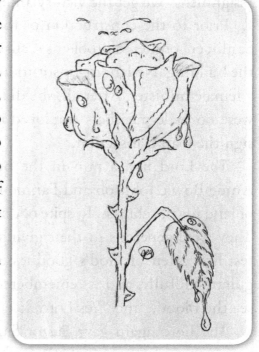

Chapter 7

IN HER OWN WORDS

BY THE LATE EVANGELIST LILLIE B. SANLIN

The following is an article given to the Faith Temple Pentecostal Church Mission Family in 1972:

A few months ago I was awaken in the wee hours of the morning. As the Spirit of the Lord said to me, "Have not I commanded thee, be strong and of a good courage. Be not afraid, neither be thou dismayed, for the Lord thy God is with thee whither-so-ever thou goest." How wonderful it is to be encouraged and strengthened by the Lord.

A few years ago while driving on the highway; my trip became long and wearisome. Before I could realize it, I went to sleep at the wheel. When I awakened I was going down a steep hill. I cried out to the Lord to save me. Immediately, as if someone said, "cut the wheel," I obeyed. I hit a tree and the car came to a stop. My head was cut and the artery in my right knee. As I was recovering, the Lord spoke to me, and had me to know my life was reserved to do a work for Him.

A few days later as I was praying, a fog entered my room, and a voice said unto me, "eat the roll, the whole roll, and speak unto the house of Israel, for they are a rebellious house." In keeping my charge which the Lord commissioned me to do; I find it a pleasure to put forth an effort in building a house unto the Lord.

Throughout my many years of ministering, I have witnessed a great move of God and seen many miracles wrought. I can truly say without a doubt, "Jesus Christ is the same yesterday, and today, and forever." (Hebrews 13:8).

As President and Chairman of this movement, I shall do my utmost to promote holiness in the fear of the Lord. I shall stand firm, and speak the words of Christ as they are written in The Holy Bible. This is not my calling by choice. For a few years I ran from the Lord. Take my word, you cannot hide from God. Everywhere I went He was there.

He brought me to nothing. He caused me to see myself. I lost everything I owned. I hardly had descent clothes to wear. I was still running from the Lord. Then I began to see crowds of people rushing toward me with funny faces, and their hands lifted. I saw them many times during the day and at night also. One night I surrendered and cried out to God, "Lord I will go where-so-ever you send me, and I will say what you want me to say."

From that moment unto this moment, I have been at peace with my maker. I find great joy in sounding the trumpet, and warning men, women, boys and girls to repent of their sins, and prepare their soul for the return of our Lord and Savior,

Jesus Christ. "Repent and be baptized, every one of you in the name of Jesus Christ for the remission of sins, and ye shall receive the gift of the Holy Ghost." (Acts 2:38).

*   *   *

Below are excerpts from two tracts written by Pastor Sanlin-c1973:

Am I My Brother's Keeper?

Those were the words of Cain after he had slain (killed) his brother Abel (Genesis 4). Abel was killed because he had found favor with God in bringing a choice offering unto Him. It pleases the Lord when we offer unto Him our best.

Through my years of ministering, I have witnessed the same spirit working among the people of God that moved in the heart of Cain (the spirit of jealousy). Cain and Abel were in the field when this sin was put into action, but the eyes of the Lord are in every place, beholding the evil and the good. (Proverbs 15:3)

How many of our brothers, and sisters in Christ Jesus have given their lives to Jesus, put forth untimely efforts to win souls, and to make proof of their ministry? Then, that same spirit that used Cain to destroy his brother's life begins working among the spiritual brothers and sisters. It is trying to destroy the life of those who have dedicated their lives to the Lord. God said unto Cain, "What hast thou done? The voice of thy brother's blood crieth unto me from the ground." (Genesis 4:10)

Cain's sin had come to the light. For there is nothing covered that shall not be revealed, neither hid, that shall not be known. (St. Matthew 10:26). Every secret plan, underhanded scheme or trick, shall be revealed in the Day of Judgment.

The spirit of jealousy is as cruel as the grave. (Song of Solomon 8:6) The spirit of jealousy is a driving spirit to the degree that it causes one not to rest, and be content. This spirit of the Devil will give a person the desire to take revenge without considering that the act could destroy their own soul. Beware of the sin of jealousy. He that covereth his sins shall not prosper, but he who confesseth and forsaketh them shall have mercy. (Proberbs 28:13)

* * *

You Can Be Healed

We serve a mighty God who will never fail us. By His Spirit miracles are wrought. Lay aside every doubt and fear, and take hold to faith, for it is faith that moves the Lord. Now the Lord is that Spirit: and where the Spirit of the Lord is, there is liberty. (2 Corinthians 3:17). The Spirit of the Lord will drive out sickness and diseases, for demons cannot rule the Lord.

I was a victim of cancer. It had spread throughout my entire body. Even the crown of my head was soft like mud. Yet I refused to let fear grip my heart, for I knew in whom I believed. Jesus, who is the head of my life, was my only physician, and He diagnosed my case. I am a faith teacher, and I felt that now was my time to exercise the faith I taught others.

During this trial, I taught the Word with joy and preached with even greater joy. Months and months passed, and my body became very weak. Yet, I kept going in Jesus' name, waiting on the God of my salvation.

Finally, one day it happened as I was in my friend's home preparing to leave. I said to her, "Let us pray." As we were praying, the Lord whispered and said, "Lay your hands on your body, and rebuke that demon of cancer." As I obeyed the voice of the Lord, it seemed like heaven opened up. The Spirit of the living God came into the room in a mighty way, and touched me from head to feet. I can say, "With His stripes, I was healed." Jesus Christ is the same yesterday, and today, and forever. (Hebrews 13:8). For we walk by faith, not by sight. (2 Corinthians 5:7). Yes, you too can be healed!

GO BACK AND COMPLETE
THE PROCESS

(INTERPRETATION OF A DREAM BY PASTOR SANLIN)

Several months after I received Jesus as Lord and Savior ("got saved"); I had a very disturbing dream. Parkway Plaza on Highway 12 West was under construction during this time in c1971-1972.

In the dream, one of the buildings on the lower west end had the appearance of a gymnasium with lots of aluminum bleachers. People were already seated when I walked in, and others were continuing to enter the double glass doors. I found a seat on the first bleacher and sat down about midway. Immediately, a funny feeling overcame me so I began to look around the gym. I noticed a huge woman sitting on the very top bleacher. I wondered how in the world she managed to get way up there. Thoughts began to race through my mind, and I said to myself, "I sure hope there is no emergency in here tonight because if that huge woman falls, she will fall on top of me."

It seemed the basketball game was about to start when I heard a loud noise behind me. Something was happening! People began jumping from the bleachers above to the floor. When I turned to see what was going on, the huge woman was falling in my direction. I had no time to run as she fell so quickly, and I felt the impact of her weight as she covered my body entirely. This cannot be happening to me, I thought. I am too young to die. I just got saved a few months ago, and God would not let this happen to me!

When the huge woman covered my body it appeared we became one individual. Breathing was becoming difficult as I was being suffocated by the weight. As a last effort, I tried to wiggle from underneath her but with no success. I could hear people saying, "Call 911, are there any medical persons here? Does anybody know CPR?"

I could see people exiting the building through the same glass doors I had entered even though I was trapped underneath the woman. Some of the people were scared, and others were crying as they were ushered out the door so the medical team could work on the huge woman. No one in the building seemed to know who the woman was.

When I saw the first responders I started screaming, "Get me out, I am under her. Get me out!" Then I realized that no one could hear me. "Turn her over," I yelled. "You will see me if you turn her body over!" Again, no one even heard me and she was finally pronounced dead. I saw several men lift the huge woman from the floor to a stretcher. As they lifted her up, I came along also because it seemed we were one individual. They moved the stretcher to the hallway of the now empty building, and somehow I knew they were awaiting the arrival of the funeral home directors.

I observed the first responders also exiting the building and locking the doors. This was too odd. You don't intentionally leave a dead body in a building like that! Why was not the coroner called? Why they seemed to omit some of the protocols was beyond my comprehension. "I am dying and no one wants to help me," I thought. "God, please help me," I prayed. After the plea, I tried wiggling myself again in a last effort to get free from the woman. This time I was making progress. Finally, I was free but the body still lay on the stretcher.

As I approached the double doors, I remembered seeing the first responders lock them when they left the building. To my surprise when I pushed on the door, it opened and I went out.

From Parkway Plaza I only needed to take the Golf Course Road (the next right turn), and walk about one and a half miles to Dorothy, my sister's house. Instead of walking I ran. Upon arriving, I knocked on the door, and no one answered. I went to the window to the right, while standing on the porch, and started banging on it. No one looked up even though I could see my family crying through the window. Somehow I knew they were crying over my death. But I was not dead! I had survived, and was banging repeatedly on a window that would not even break. I was screaming to them, "It is me, Lillie, I am not dead!" Still, no one looked in my direction or heard the banging.

I must get to Mom's (Pastor Sanlin) house, I thought. She will tell my family I am not dead! Now I started running again without even feeling exhausted. I ran about another five miles to Mom's home in town and I began knocking repeatedly on the door. Mom opened the door, but had a very strange look on her face. Immediately I began babbling. "Mom, my family thinks I am dead. Please call and tell them I am alive. They were crying at home and could not hear me knocking on the door or window. Please tell them Mom, please!"

She looked at me very sternly, and pointed in the direction from which I had just come. She simply said, "Go back and complete the process." "But you do not understand, if I go back I will have to crawl back underneath that huge woman, and then I will certainly die," I responded. Without moving her hand she repeated, "Go back."

If Mom does not believe me, I have no one else to turn to I thought. Feeling hopeless, with head hung down, I moved off her porch, and walked slowly toward Parkway Plaza. When I pushed on the door of the building it opened as if never locked. The huge woman still lay on the stretcher, and I managed to crawl back underneath her. Within a few minutes breathing became difficult and I felt myself die. The dream is now over.

For the next three weeks I lived in torment. If I saw an over-weight woman on my side of the street, I crossed over to the other side. I felt that if I ever saw that huge woman the dream would materialize, and my life would be over.

After much mental stress, I decided to share the dream with Mom. She said, "Daughter, why did you wait so long? The dream is of a spiritual nature. The huge woman represents the weight of sins in your life. I instructed you to go back, and complete the process because you, like us all, must die out to sin." The Apostle Paul states in Romans 6:14, Sin shall have no more dominion over you. He also states in 1 Corinthians 6:11, But such were some of you . . .

What a relief it was when God gave Mom the interpretation of my dream. Daniel said to King Nebuchadnezar in Daniel 2:28, But there is a God in heaven that revealeth secret things (read entire book of Daniel). Joseph stood before Pharoah in Genesis 41:15-16 and stated . . . it is not in me: God shall give Pharoah an answer of peace.

I believe God anointed the Late Pastor Sanlin to operate in the nine gifts of the Spirit (1 Corinthians 12:5-11). She took no credit, or honor for herself, but gave it back to God. I know because I was there. An eyewitness to what God will do with a yielded vessel after He places His anointing upon their life.

Chapter 9

YOU'RE LOOKING AT A MIRACLE!

1973

After graduating from high school I moved to New Brunswick, New Jersey and thought life was wonderful. Nevertheless, right before Christmas my mother became very ill so I quit my job (I was not eligible for family medical leave). I came home for a few months to help care for her. Momma came first, and I could always get another job. My plan was to return to New Brunswick in early May 1971.

In April 1971, a peculiar rash about the size of a quarter coin developed on the back of my neck. Momma and I were concerned about it spreading so I went to our local family doctor. That doctor referred me to a dermatologist at University Hospital, Jackson, Mississippi, for further evaluation. The doctor thought the rash might originate from dust or grass, so they played tic-tac-toe on my left arm. Every thirty minutes I was administered five allergy test with a needle (a total of 50) that pierced just underneath the skin. No allergies were noted after those tests, and some other extensive testing was done.

The University physician suggested I see another dermatologist outside the state of Mississippi. He noted my problem might be a type of food allergy, and they had no test to give at that time for food allergies. The physician also stated that I had been given their best care over the last two months, but we declined the additional treatment.

The rash was not easily noticeable, but I knew it was there. Then I went to that life-changing Bible Class taught by Pastor Sanlin. As mentioned earlier, from that time forth, life as I had once known it was never the same. I was really enjoying the peace of mind I obtained from the Lord. Life had real meaning now that my mind had been transformed.

Pastor Sanlin walked by faith and trusted God to meet all her needs. She in turn admonished the church to do likewise. I did not request prayer for the rash early on but did later. So now I was growing in the Lord, even though the rash was growing also. While waiting on God for deliverance, my sense of smell "simply vanished." Then in September 1971, a personal condition in my body developed which was most perplexing. I realized unclean spirits were trying to discourage me from trusting God, but now it appeared they wanted to kill me as well.

I knew Pastor Sanlin, and others were praying for me even though my condition was not improving. The rash had spread to my face, scalp, arms, hands and lower legs. Some people at church were skeptical about shaking my hand, but I did not blame them. What if the rash was contagious?

My mother told me that a deacon from the church she attended stated that if I was his daughter, he would not let me go out into the public. That statement hurt, but only confirmed what I already knew. I looked awful! Sometimes I would compare my skin to that of a frog, and thought the frog looked so much better. The Devil will magnify anything if you allow him to do so.

Mom continued to pray, lay hands on me, and offer counsel regarding proper care of my skin to help eliminate the spread of the rash. There were times in the service when the anointing of God filled the church. Following the leading of the Holy Ghost, Pastor Sanlin would call different people up for prayer, including me. Often, they would get their deliverance right away while my condition remained the same. That was quite baffling because I knew from experience that God's anointing brought deliverance.

I started quoting scriptures on healing, became more stable in my faith walk, and was expecting that "any day now miracle." One year passed and I still believed God for my healing. Two years had passed and I was 21 years old, and engaged to be married to James Rufus Miller in September 1973.

One night, May 1973, we traveled to Preston, Mississippi, for a fellowship service where Mom was the guest speaker. On the way to church we stopped by a convenience store. Mom knew the stores would be closed by the time we left the service, so she advised us to purchase snacks at that time. I recall getting a bag of pork skins and something to drink.

We had a glorious time in the service and eventually started back home. Everyone was talking about the service, and how the Spirit of the Lord had moved as they ate their snacks. After consuming a few skins, I began coughing repeatedly. I tried to quiet the coughing by drinking some soda but it only made matters worse. Mom prayed for me, but I coughed periodically all the way back to Kosciusko.

Since we knew we would be returning home late, some of the young people had planned to stay overnight. This meant I would be sleeping with Mom in her bedroom, as the sofa sleeper would accommodate Sisters Delois and Wardean Kennedy.

By now the coughing had almost ceased, then upon going to bed the coughing returned. I knew Mom was extremely tired from the drive and ministering too. The annoying cough only complicated matters, and Mom finally dozed off to sleep. I continued to cough periodically. Then, in the early hours of the morning, Mom turned over toward me, placed her hand on my forehead and said, "Satan, I rebuke you in Jesus' name." She returned back to her original sleeping position as if never awakened. The coughing ceased immediately and never returned.

Later that morning I discovered that not only had God delivered me from the coughing, but I was also healed from the personal condition in my body that had lingered on for almost two years. Praise God for victory at last! . . . The effectual fervent prayers of a righteous man availeth much. (James 5:16) God may not always come when we think he should, but he is always on time.

A few more weeks passed, and for the first time in almost two years, I could smell toast cooking at Momma's house. From that time forth, my sense of smell improved and I was truly blessing God for my healing. It was my time for total deliverance! The Virgin Mary's response to the message she had received from the angel regarding the Savior's birth took on a new meaning for me. In a different sense, I too could say, "He that is mighty hath done to me great things, and holy is his name." (Luke 1:49)

In June 1973, I was awakened around 6:30 A.M. at Momma's house. It felt like someone was blowing air directly in my face. Something was happening! I could feel some of the bumps on my face bursting as if someone had penetrated them with a pin, leaving a cool sensation all over my face. I jumped up to look in the mirror on the dresser. The horrible skin condition was vanishing quickly before my eyes.

I called my mother to show her what was happening. Then I asked her to call my sister, Mary, who lived next door, to bring her Polaroid camera to take a snap shot of my face. I had wanted proof to show others what my skin condition actually looked like in case they did not believe my testimony. Prior to the miracle taking place, I had no desire to have a picture taken of my face.

Now it only took Mary a few minutes to come over, and I asked her to get a good close up snap shot quickly. The bumps were evaporating so fast that by the time she took the picture, God had completely healed me! The picture only exposed a close up view of my face with clear skin. What we were looking at was a divine miracle from God!

James, half-brother to Jesus, speaks encouraging words in James 5:13-16, Is any among you afflicted? Let him pray. Is any merry? Let him sing psalms. Is any sick among you? Let him call for the elders of the church; and let them pray over him, anointing him with oil in the name of the Lord: and the prayer of faith shall save the sick, and the Lord shall raise him up; and if he have committed sins, they shall be forgiven him. The effectual fervent prayer of a righteous man availeth much.

I thank God for all who prayed for me during that trying time, but especially Pastor Sanlin. She constantly interceded on my behalf to the Lord. She taught the church to "have faith in God." She is gone but the fruit remains. So when you see me, "You're looking at an individual who has been healed by the power of God, a divine miracle!"

Chapter 10

UNCLEAN SPIRITS ARE REAL!

(PASTOR SANLIN'S TEACHINGS ARE CHALLENGED)
RUSSELL'S STORY 1975-1976

To everything there is a season and a time to every purpose under the heaven: a time to be born . . . (Ecclesiastes 3:1-2), and then came Russell in 1975. He was my second child and first son. Russell was a healthy baby with a lot of thick, black, curly hair. It was the kind of hair you wanted your daughters to have. His facial complexion was really smooth and chocolate. Russell was so handsome with a captivating smile that stole your heart, and people just loved to hold him.

He was a very sweet baby during the day, but at night he was a crying nightmare. I would sing to him while attempting to rock him to sleep. Yet nothing seemed to make a difference with Russell at night. Before moving to Louisiana I would stay overnight at my Momma's home. Then around 8:30 P.M., Russell cried so much that Momma and I would take turns pacing the floor, trying to console him. Ritually, before daybreak he would fall asleep. This cycle repeated itself nightly till he was about four months old.

Russell had been examined by a pediatrician, but no problems were noted. The doctor seemed to think in time he would grow out of the crying spells. It really did not make much sense because overall Russell had a good disposition. Anyhow, I was almost a nervous wreck trying to figure that child out. Not even Asfidity (medication for babies with colic causing crying spells) worked on him.

I was privileged to work closely with Mom from 1971 to early 1976. I served as Church Secretary which involved typing business correspondence. Whenever work was to be done, I would stay overnight. Since James was working in Louisiana, I knew I had time to complete the work. Arrangements were made for me to spend a Sunday night at her home so we could get an early start on Monday morning.

After church that Sunday evening, a few of the young people came over to the trailer. Mom was talking to us as we sat around the kitchen table. I do not remember the exact conversation, but Brother David Luckett said, "Mom, would you repeat that again?" She replied, "When Mom is talking I expect you all to pay attention. I am not putting up with any demons in this house." Secretly, I thought Mom was being pretty harsh as Brother David only asked for the sentence to be repeated. Then Brother David said, "I am sorry Mom, but I got distracted." Mom proceeded to repeat the sentence, and I am sure the rest of us silently committed to give her our full attention (not wanting to risk getting that type of rebuke).

It was at that moment that I realized what Russell's problem really was. He had a crying demon and I did not want Mom to find out. Mom taught the mothers that we were the parents, and should be able to control our own children. Therefore, I thought not being able to control Russell's crying episodes was going to make me look like an incompetent parent. The Devil did not want me to even acknowledge that I was in the right place for deliverance. All I was concerned about was how I was going to keep Russell from crying most of the night, and it was already 8:30 P.M.

Around 9:00 P.M., Mom announced that everyone should go to bed since we had a lot of work to do on Monday. I agreed, and around 9:30 P.M. I placed Russell very close to me so whenever he wiggled I could grab him quickly. I watched the clock as the time approached 10:00 P.M., 11:00 P.M. Then 2:00 A.M. arrived, 4:00 A.M., and finally round 5:30 A.M., I decided to stop watching, and waiting for Russell to start crying and go to sleep. When 8:00 A.M. came, I was so exhausted. I had spent the majority of the night trying to keep watch over Russell when God had already delivered him.

Mom's statement to Brother David, "I am not putting up with any demon in this house," had been heard by the unclean crying spirit too. That demon had to be subject to her statement spoken with authority. From that time forth Russell was delivered, and I never dealt with that unnecessary crying demon again. Praise the Lord!

As parents, we need to understand that Satan's attacks are not always directed toward us. He hates our children because he knows they too can wreak havoc on his kingdom. King Solomon urges us to "Train up a child in the way he should go." (Proverbs 22:6). Parents, guardians or care givers, it is our responsibility to point our children in the path they should go. If we allow unclean spirits to go undetected in our children, as the child grows, so that spirit will grow. You see Satan has a "grow up plan too." It is not a shame to acknowledge our children need deliverance. We must face the facts, and call that spirit by name. Don't wait till they are teenagers.

Watch the pattern of the enemy. If you look closely you'll see the pattern. Ask God to reveal unto you what is really going on with that child. You might say they're stubborn just like I was growing up. That's a spirit! Call it by name and deal with that spirit now so you will not be sorry later. Guard your home with prayer and consecration. Watch the company you keep, and the television programs you allow to enter your home. Unclean spirits are real, and they are looking for vessels to use. Yes, we have an adversary, Satan, and God has given us the authority to cast out unclean spirits. Use what God has given you. Plead the blood of Jesus!

A few years ago the Holy Ghost spoke to my spirit and said, "Satan's plan is to cheat our children out of a fighting chance." He does this through spirits of molestation, neglect, physical abuse, emotional scarring (which often results in low self-esteem) and etcetera. Unclean spirits want to cripple our children at an early age, decreasing their possibility of reaching their fullest potential in God and the secular world.

Many years have passed since that encounter with a crying demon, and Russell is an anointed, ordained minister of the gospel, and a strong disciplinarian. He preaches and teaches the word of God without compromise. Russell is also a gifted sketching artist on the verge of a break through. Pray for Minister Miller and his family as they fight the good fight of faith.

* * *

JASON'S STORY
1981-1982

November 14, 1976 was a day truly implanted in my memory. That was the date the twins were born, Jason and Jarome. They were double the joy and double the challenge. "Boys will be boys," and mine were no exception. They loved playing, whether it was in the house or outside in the backyard. For a while I believe their feelings were mixed up. If Jason fell down, and scraped his knee, Jarome would cry and vice versa. Though they were termed identical twins, I could tell them apart most of the time. One thing though distinctly set them apart, Jason had more serious accidents than Jarome.

Each year between November and January something would happen to Jason. His injuries sometimes caused a visit to the doctor or emergency room. The accidents became more noticeable when he was about five years old in 1981.

Late one afternoon he and his younger sister, Lili, had been playing in the hallway. I had warned them to stop running, but the temptation to do so must have been unbearable. I came into the hallway to scold them, but witnessed a head on collision instead. Lili appeared to be alright, but Jason began crying as he had received the greater force from the impact.

Both children were corrected, and sent to their room to play. Since Jason was still crying, he was restricted from playing, and had to sit and watch the others, even though he had no visible swelling or knots.

When bed time arrived, James and I decided to keep Jason awake for a while longer. This was a precaution in case he had a mild head concussion from the earlier collision. Around 10:00 P.M. Jason was allowed to go to sleep. Around 11:00 P.M. I went to check on him and was shocked. Jason had a light brown facial complexion so discoloration showed up easily. His face was so swollen you could hardly tell where his left eye was located, and bruising was very visible. So off to Charity Hospital's emergency room in New Orleans, Louisiana, he and I go.

Once inside the emergency room area, the first person we met appeared to be intoxicated with an awful looking black eye. The man said to Jason as we walked by, "Looks like somebody stung you real good, Buddy." We kept walking as I paid little attention to the man, and wondered why he even made the statement.

Soon it was Jason's turn to see the doctor. When I attempted to escort him to the examination room the nurse asked me to remain in the waiting area, noting he would be back soon. About fifteen minutes later Jason returned with the nurse who stated the doctor would see him shortly. A few minutes passed and Jason was called again. I stood up to go with him and was told to remain in the waiting area.

Shortly thereafter, a policeman walked through the waiting area, and it appeared he glanced slightly at me even though the room was crowded. The officer went into one of the examination rooms and stayed a while. I did not know till later that he was actually in the same room as Jason.

Jason came back again with the nurse who said a few more tests need to be run. By now I have put two and two together. "Oh My God," I thought, "they think I am a child abuser!" That is probably what that drunk man meant by his statement. By now the nurse has returned for Jason again. I stood to go with him and she said, "We will call you when needed." Visibly frustrated, I went into the hallway and said to the nurse, "Two times you have examined my son without me being present, and I want to know what's going on. He will not be examined again without me!"

Then the doctor and policeman came into the hallway. The doctor approached me and proceeded to say they were following procedure when a case looks like child abuse. I replied, "Child abuse! You do not even know what happened!" The doctor responded, "That is why we talk to the child alone first, without the parent. Then hopefully, we can get the truth, and it seems as if someone put the words in his mouth regarding what took place. When asked what happened, your son stated, my sister fell me down."

"Doctor, he and his younger sister were running in the hallway and collided. Jason is only five years old, do you expect him to speak English like I do?" was my response. "No, but if a case looks like child abuse, we treat it as such until the facts are gathered," he said.

So yes, I did escort Jason for his final eye examination, and the doctor found no real problems except that his face was badly bruised from the impact. He also noted that this case was probably not child abuse, and after several days the bruising should clear up. I was so glad when we were finally able to leave that emergency room. I vowed to never return there again and I did not. I understood the doctor's precaution, but I also knew Jason was not a victim of child abuse.

On the way out of the emergency room, I decided to take Jason to the bathroom as we had a forty minute drive back home. As we attempted to enter the bathroom door, we met a young girl trying to come out. She was in a wheel chair, and had a black eye, one arm was in a sling, and a cast had been placed on one leg. "Oh Lord," I thought, "now that looks like child abuse."

When Jason was six years old (January 1982), he encountered another serious accident. The backyard where all the children were playing (six by now) was big. The children were really having a good time playing outside on that nice winter day. Then I heard Jason crying. Through the kitchen back door I could see Jason lying on the ground, and holding his left arm. He had managed to locate, and fall on a small triangular piece of brick embedded in the ground that James couldn't dig up, although he had tried. The children played in the backyard often, and you had to really look hard to see it, as it was level with the ground and grass. Somehow Jason managed to find that spot!

One look at that arm and off to the local doctor's office in Marrero, Louisiana, we go. Thank God it was before five o'clock, and the office was still open. We arrived and Jason was seen immediately. X-rays revealed his arm was broken, and had it been a little worse, surgery would have been necessary to reset it. A cast was put on and Jason was finally consoled. After he was given several lollipops, we started home.

As I thought and prayed about Jason's situation, the Spirit of the Lord reminded me of Russell's encounter at four months of age. The Holy Ghost said that a "pattern" had been established. You see, during certain periods Jason encountered accidents, and this was nothing but an "accident prone spirit." Oftentimes, things we term "normal" may just be the opposite. Sometimes, we say they are just naturally clumsy. Are they? After that conversation with the Holy Ghost, I knew that I had to address that accident prone demon.

The next day after the cast was put on, Jason and I went shopping for a size seven long sleeve shirt to accommodate his new arm size, as it was still winter time. The Holy Ghost had already instructed me to talk to Jason on a child's level first, and then address the unclean spirit.

I proceeded to tell Jason that he was the only one of the children having a lot of accidents. Also, he needed to try, and be more careful when playing, because whenever he got hurt it made us sad. We loved him, and he was such a big boy, but we needed him to help us keep him safe. With the biggest Miller smile on his face he said he would try harder to be more careful. Then I said, "Jason, I am finished talking to you. Now I must talk to the spirit that makes you have accidents. If I use the word demon or Satan, I am not talking to you. Do you understand me son?" Though only six years old, he assured me he understood what I was saying.

Now it was time to address that unclean spirit: Satan, I rebuke you in Jesus name. You unclean accident prone demon, I bind you and cast you out of Jason in Jesus name, and I forbid you to return. I plead the blood of Jesus. Jason belongs to God and you will not cause him to have another serious accident. He will play and grow as a normal child without interference from you. Now Lord, I thank you for the angels protecting, and surrounding Jason. He will not have another serious accident in Jesus name. Amen.

I will have you to know that my God kept Jason and he never had another serious accident thereafter. The next time Jason had an incident he was a grown man, and married with one child. Glory to God! Jason had been welding on his job along with another coworker. A fragment, off the metal press plate machine from the coworker's machine, cut Jason about one half inch below his right eye on the cheek bone.

Jason called me from the local emergency room and said, "Momma." I said, "What happened son?" Mothers, you know many times from the mere tone of your child's voice that something is wrong. I reminded Jason that as long as he was under my roof Satan could not touch him. He was on his own now, and must take authority over that unclean, accident prone spirit himself that was trying to return back into his life.

"Ye shall know the truth and the truth shall make you free." (John 8:32) Thank God that Pastor Sanlin had instilled the Word of God in me. She had taught about unclean spirits from the pulpit as well as sitting around the kitchen table. Those spirits were not to be feared, but the people of God should use the power given us and take authority over them. Unclean spirits are real, and take pleasure in inflicting chaos in the life of children, youth and adults, saved or unsaved. It is vital that we stay alert, and look beyond the natural for a spiritual revelation.

Remember, Satan is the real enemy. Be sober (clear-headed, aware), be vigilant (alert); because your adversary (enemy, rival) the devil, as a roaring lion, walketh about, seeking whom he may devour: whom resist steadfast in the faith . . . (1 Peter 5:8-9)

My friend, Jesus Christ is the same yesterday, and today, and forever (Hebrews 13:8). He has not given us the spirit of fear; but of power, and of love and of a sound mind (2 Timothy 1:7).

Jason has also been called into the ministry and anointed by God to preach the Good News for such a time as this. Don't be defeated! God will give you the victory over unclean spirits. He will show Himself mighty on your behalf.

Chapter 11

THE MILLER CHILDREN

On September 21, 1973, I was married to my teenage sweetheart, James Rufus Miller, and we lived in McCool, Mississippi for about two years. We were the first couple from the Faith Temple ministry to be married, but while engaged we never dated. We only talk briefly at church because when I got saved, "you were careful not to let your good be evil spoken of." So dating was not encouraged but frowned upon.

Before salvation came I loved James dearly. When he proposed to me in June 1973, (two years after I got saved) I expected that former love I once had for him to resurface, but it did not. Therefore, I had to grow to love James as my husband rather than a brother in the Lord. It was indeed a challenge but when "real love" came, I loved him unconditionally and my "for better or for worse" was tested indeed. Still, after thirteen years of marriage James and I separated for the last time, and he divorced me in 1993. The children that were born as a result of that marriage are so precious and I love them deeply. They are my gifts from the Lord and they take good care of their mother.

"We are in this together!" That was a household phrase as of December 1986. I had to remind the children often that somehow by the grace of God, everything was going to be alright. I was a single parent now, and we had to work together for the welfare of all.

I got my bluff in early with the children as I needed to build on the foundation regarding discipline that James had in place. The following was a portion of my message to them:

Unfortunately, your father and I are no longer living in the same home. I expect you to give me the same respect you gave him. I will not tell you repeatedly to obey my instructions. We will love and respect each other. No matter how upset you are with me, if the Lord blesses, when we meet in the morning you will say "Good morning." We do not slam doors in this house, we do not fight each other, and you will obey the rules that govern this home. If you do not believe what I am saying try me! You will live long enough to regret it. Remember, you are all the children I have and I cannot replace you. I love you now and always, so let's make this new life work.

Yes, the Miller children, two daughters and four sons. God knows I did not raise any angels but neither did I have to bond any of them out of jail. They were PKs (preacher's kids) but they had their own identity.

Charlene "Charla" Miller-Nash was born July 3, 1974. She was a pretty little plump baby, with big cheeks, an adorable smile, curly hair and a gentle spirit. She was training ground for James and me as young parents. Regrettably, Charlene had to endure all the blunders first time parents make. She was a sweet child that matured so fast, and just enjoyed helping around the house. Even as a child her little take-charge spirit was quite noticeable.

Charlene was musically inclined early in life. When she was about two and a half years old, it was evident that she had been anointed by God as a vocalist. Her favorite song was "I'm Bound for Mt. Zion," recorded by Margaret Allison and the Angelic Gospel Singers. When she sang that song my mother thought she was an angel in disguise, and whatever "Charla" wanted, "Charla" got.

When she was about five years old, we got her a small keyboard for Christmas. She would create her own music and it sounded really good. One day I lay in bed sick. Charlene brought her keyboard into my bedroom, and announced she was going to play me her "Friendship Song." When she finished playing the Lord had healed me of whatever my problem was through her anointed music. I recall getting up and completing my unfinished tasks.

Charlene was always eager to learn and loved helping with her younger sister, Lili. From the time Lili was about one and a half years old, Charlene tried to do everything for her. When Lili was about two and a half years old she was eating a piece of chocolate candy, and decided to feed Charlene's tape player some of the candy. Definitely, the tape player was ruined, and Charlene brought Lili to me. She said, "Momma, here is your baby back" and thereafter, she rarely assisted in caring for Lili.

Charlene matured into a beautiful, intelligent young lady who adapted to change easily. God has anointed her as a vocalist, and she is especially gifted in the area of child care education. Charlene attended Tougaloo College, Tougaloo, Mississippi, and Mississippi Valley State University, Itta Bena, Mississippi. Charlene is the mother of two sons, Tylaor Price and Jiheim Nash.

James Russell Miller was born November 22, 1975. He also exhibited a "take charge spirit." You were given an introduction to him in "Unclean Spirits are Real-Russell's Story." I mentioned earlier that the children had to abide by the house rules. Well, one day I came home late from work around 8:00 P.M. I actually was off at 4:00 P.M., but had some errands to run, and several church related home visits.

When I arrived home, Russell was waiting for me in the living room. He said, with a certain tone of voice I had not heard before, "Mom, we need to talk. You told us we had to be home by a definite time. If we are running late it is required that we call home because you would be worried. Well, I think that same rule should apply to you too. We also get worried when you're not here by a certain time."

I was speechless for a minute. I didn't know whether to resort to the "authoritative parent mode" or just submit. So I said, "Okay," I'll abide by that rule too. I'm sorry I had you worried." This gave Russell the reassurance that his opinion mattered. I also realized that Russell was really maturing into quite a young man even though he was only in the tenth grade.

Russell is a very intelligent, hardworking young man with that same smooth chocolate complexion. He attended Holmes Community College, Goodman, Mississippi, and East Central Community College, Decatur, Mississippi. Russell is married to Candice (Harris), and they have three children, Wandre' Harris, Marquea and Danye' Miller.

Jason Lamont Miller was born November 14, 1976. He is the oldest twin with a light brown facial complexion, a smile that lights up the room and those well-defined Miller eyes. When he was born he had so many Indian features with straight glossy black hair. He is tall, handsome and has a business man profile in appearance. You were introduced to him in "Unclean Spirits are Real-Jason's Story."

The Lord has blessed Jason to overcome so much and even now, God isn't finished with him. Jason matured into a very intelligent young man, like all my sons. He attended Holmes Community College, Goodman, Mississippi, and earned a certificate in Welding in May 1996. Miller Installation was his first business venture. Jason has been blessed with three children, Jamall, Jy'Lisha and Joi Miller.

Jarome Lamar Miller was born November 14, 1976. He is the youngest twin with a light brown facial complexion, "puppy dog eyes," tall and handsome. That Miller smile will simply steal your heart. Jarome also has a great sense of humor. As a child, people just loved him because he was the smaller of the twins, and they felt he needed extra attention. As an adult, he is greatly adored by the family.

Jarome is definitely gifted by God in articulation. He is the only one of the children that could talk one's socks off, and the person would not even know the socks were missing. Jarome blossomed into quite a young man. He always made sure I had spending money just for me and I appreciate it. I never tire of the poems, flowers, gifts or phone calls as he is one of a kind.

I remember the car accident that resulted in Jarome being hospitalized when he was about ten years old. The older siblings talked him into going to the store across from the school for candy. I had warned them not to go, but they knew he was not in the room when I gave those instructions. He was their little guinea pig but Jarome also had much to profit from the trip as well.

When I arrived to pick up the children from after school tutoring they told me Jarome had been hit by a car and had been taken by ambulance to the hospital. I must have run every red light in town trying to get to the hospital. The Lord blessed and after an over-night hospital stay for observation, he was alright. Jarome still has that missing spot of hair on his scalp where he landed on the pavement, but God preserved his life, and for that I am grateful.

Watching him develop into such an intelligent and handsome young man has been rewarding. Jarome is a 2000 graduate of Meridian Community College, Meridian, Mississippi, and also attended Mississippi Valley State

University, Itta Bena, Mississippi. He is a 2010 graduate of America Trade Institute, Garland, Texas, and received certification in Heating Ventilating and Air Conditioning. Jarome is married to Deshona (Lewis), and they have one daughter, Lauren Miller. Jarome is also blessed to have two other daughters, Jarah Miller and Helen Moore.

Lili Brietta Miller Hardin-Swanigan was born January 15, 1978. She was my last daughter and "Black Barbie." Her smooth chocolate facial complexion, full head of thick curly hair, that "runway walk," and "strong will" made her a challenge indeed!

She was destined for greatness, but we had a lot of drama to overcome first. I believe she had a question that needed a full explanation to something every day. With six children it seems there was never enough quality time to go around, and Lili noticed that right away. She would say periodically, "We don't have a mother, the church has our mother." Lili did not understand that I had to balance my time between home, church, and work.

I listened attentively to her grievance and then replied, "I have a plan. From now on when I have home visitations during the week, I'm taking you with me. Since you'll be accompanying me, it will help me to limit the amount of time I spend in one home. On the way to the next home, we can talk about your day. When all the visitations are complete, we'll eat out and get ice cream before returning home."

I believe for every problem there is a practical solution, and ice cream just enhances the solution. So Lili accompanied me for a short time and could see first-hand what I was dealing with. I let her decide when enough was enough.

Lili is a Minister of the Gospel now and asks me for advice on how she can manipulate home, children, church, and full-time employment. She fully understands better now that it's her struggle to find balance, with children who always seem to need a little more time with her. God is blessing and she's doing an excellent job.

When Lili was three months old she developed a terrible rash in her face and scalp. The doctors termed it "cradle cap," but I had never seen a case that involved the facial area as well as the scalp. After the second office visit, the doctor advised me to daily soak her scalp in olive oil then wash it out later. I was so happy to be able to use the olive oil, because I also used it for prayer oil. Other medication was also prescribed. When the Lord completely healed Lili, there were no scars in her face as a result of the awful rash. God is good all the time, for he certainly extended his grace unto her.

Being a "strong willed" child earned Lili plenty of disciplinary measures. On one occasion (as a teen) I had whipped her, and then she was grounded for a few months. She was upset and so was I! When I punished the children, rarely did I modify it. On this particular occasion, after the discipline we both went to bed.

During the course of the night I just could not sleep. I prayed about the matter but still could not sleep. Early that morning the Holy Spirit spoke and said, "There is nothing wrong with your daughter that was not wrong with you. She is similar to the old Lillie, and you do not like what you see." I had to agree with the Lord one hundred percent. I then debated mentally as to whether I should apologize to Lili for being a bit harsh.

At that minute, someone knocked on the door, while opening it at the same time. As I stood up, it was Lili with out-stretched arms saying, "Momma, I am so sorry." We both stood there crying, and embracing each other while apologizing. I shared with her what the Holy Spirit had spoken, and things got much better between us. Lili has two children, Nabretta and Merthia Hardin. She attended Hinds Community College, Raymond, Mississippi, Southwest Technical Community School, and University of Memphis, Memphis, Tennessee.

I have learned over the years that parenting is never easy, and that saying "I am sorry" when it is needed does not minimize who you are as the parent. Let's face it, parenting is a tough job! We have to pray, learn from the mistakes we make, learn from others' mistakes, read, observe, and seek wise counsel from the aged. There are no manuals for successful parenting that fits all children. If you are parenting children from birth to college age, may the Lord grant you grace, mercy, and wisdom for the days ahead.

Rufus Tafton Miller was born February 18, 1980. He is known simply as "T" and is the last of the Miller children. He definitely has the Miller eyes, a broad, "steal your heart smile," a brown facial complexion, tall, handsome, and has a distinctive beard. In my presence, he was the one with a consistent sweet and gentle spirit, but I have a feeling his behavior was different among his siblings.

"T" sometimes struggled to make good grades, but was determined to do so. Even now he still embraces challenge. "T" did not require a lot of discipline, but he could be mischievous. When he was in the seventh grade his music teacher came to the office one day (I was employed at the same school where he attended), visibly frustrated and crying. The problem was that most of the male students were being uncooperative. They were singing their own versions of songs she was attempting to teach the class.

The teacher came to the office in tears, but only wanted me to talk with "T." She was hoping that if his behavior changed, the other boys might fall in line too. Well, I took it to another level.

I talked to the class about their disrespect and overall bad behavior. Then I disciplined (whipped) "T" in front of the class. This was not my normal routine, but it was frustrating to see the children take advantage of a teacher like that.

Of course, I talked to the teacher later about using the authority she had to bring order to her classroom. I explained to her that if the students think their behavior frustrates you, they sometimes will capitalize on it, and you'll always have turmoil. The final outcome is that they win. It was not my job to manage her class, but I wanted her and the students to succeed. After that incident, the teacher never came back to the office for behavior issues with "T."

"T" is married to Kimberly (Lum) and they have three children-Jalia McGriggs, Cameron and Adrian Miller. He is a good provider for his family, and believes in spending quality time with them as well. Since "T" is a "take charge" kind of man, Kim says she just steps back and let him be "the man."

"T" enjoys being actively involved in the "Helps Ministry" of his church in Meridian, Mississippi. He states that he doesn't mind "playing the background" as long as the job gets done.

Like the other children, watching him grow and mature into such an intelligent young man has been most rewarding. The knowledge and wisdom he has gained is astounding. I get joy out of listening to him talk about the Lord and how God has shown Himself mighty on his behalf.

Tafton attended Holmes Community College, Goodman, Mississippi, and is a 2002 graduate of ITT Technical Institute, Memphis, Tennessee. He received a degree in Drafting and Design.

Rashekia Shuntaye Simmons is my niece and adopted daughter. She was born January 8, 1987. Her biological parents are Shelia Young Simmons and Floyd P. Evans. She is short in stature, cute and cheerful. For some reason, I never thought I would have children; therefore, adoption became my dream. Shuntaye was the dream fulfilled in 2003.

Similar to Lili, her strong will earned her a lot of disciplinary measures but we survived it all, bless the Lord! Shuntaye has three children-Kabria Riley, Navaeh, and Obadiah Simmons.

I thank God for my children as they have played a vital role in "helping me to be me." I pray they will live their lives in such a way that Jesus is exalted. If it had not been for the Lord's favor, and never-ending show of mercy, I could not have endured as a single parent. Yes, I owe Him another "Thank you Jesus!"

What about you? Perhaps you are a parent or "A part of a village," the question is, can you see the Hand of God at work on your behalf?" If so, you too, owe Him a "Thank you Jesus!"

Chapter 12

WHAT ABOUT AFRICA AND CHARLES APIYO?

*I*nquiring minds want to know, What about Africa and Charles? I'm so glad you asked. Let me share my story like this:

Africa always intrigued me, and I had hoped to travel there one day. In January 1996 my Senior Pastor, the late Elder David Luckett, announced that he was finalizing a missionary trip to Nairobi, Kenya (East Africa). He announced that others were welcome to accompany him in June 1996.

That was good timing for my desire of traveling to Africa to materialize, so the church and I began making the necessary preparations. There was fundraising to organize, a passport to apply for, and an immunization card to obtain with documentation that all required vaccinations, and medication had been taken for the overseas trip.

The missionary team of five (Pastor David and Sister (Cynthia) Luckett, Mary Jones, Mother Amzie and myself) met in Chicago, Illinois. We boarded the huge Boeing 737 jet for our international flight to Africa. The flight was long but enjoyable. Finally, the jet touched down in beautiful Nairobi, Kenya. Looking out the window as the plane taxied down the runway, I saw trees shaped so different from the trees in America. Then to my surprise, through the window I could see attendants herding what looked like cows and goats.

Now it was time to leave the plane, claim the luggage, and go through airport international custom security. We had the option of exchanging our American currency or traveler's checks for the local shilling before leaving the airport. We chose not to do so as exchange rates vary from day to day. Also, the team had been informed that most businesses accepted the American dollar.

Once outside the airport, we were greeted by our pre-arranged tour guides who would transport us in two vans to our hotel located in the heart of Nairobi. If you think traffic gets congested in Jackson, Mississippi, this type of congestion was unreal. Vehicles were practically parked bumper to bumper at the airport.

As we settled in our seats, I finally said to the sisters beside me, "Whoever is driving this van has to be good to get us out of this parking space!" Then I saw the driver's face in the rear view mirror, and he looked directly at me without staring. Momentarily, there seemed to be something about him that connected with me, but I could not figure out what it was. Anyway, we were finally in Kenya and that was what mattered most.

As we made our way down the busy highway, Pastor Luckett began to chat with the two tour guides. The rest of us just looked at the scenery by night and did little talking. We arrived at our stunning New Stanley Hotel, and settled down for the night as it was late.

The next morning (Sunday) I awakened to the sights, and sounds of Nairobi. From the patio I observed the busy streets filled with people dressed in African attire, as well as the western culture look of America. The lovely flowers and trees were in full bloom, and it was hot! I observed the beautiful city landscape, and noticed that plants I struggle to grow indoors in Mississippi were thriving beautifully outdoors.

Later, we left the hotel to tour on foot the nearby area of the city. Traffic was crazy as there were few traffic lights, and crossing the street was quite an ordeal. Shoppers, especially tourists, were bartering for the best deals. Homeless people, and the less fortunate (some of which I later discovered were impostors), children and adults, positioned themselves strategically where they could encounter the most sympathizers.

As a safety precaution we had been warned not to wear jewelry, including watches, when venturing outside our hotel. Pastor Luckett had also emphasized being mindful of the counsel given us. While he was taking a nap, the ladies decided to take a walk, as Sister Luckett wanted to check out one of the nearby beauty supply stores. Again, crossing the street was frightening. One had to wait for the heavy traffic to slow down, and then attempt to cross the street together when it looked safe to do so.

Sister Luckett crossed over quickly, but the rest of us did not think we could make it. Soon, Sister Luckett uttered a muffled scream. An African teenager had snatched the watch she was wearing from her wrist, and began running in the opposite direction. We could only watch helplessly as the traffic was still heavy.

When Sister Luckett screamed, people on the sidewalk stood still. Policemen armed with machine guns were positioned in front of nearby jewelry stores in an effort to discourage robbery attempts. We had been told that those officers would shoot on the spot if they suspected wrong doing. That was the reason why Sister Luckett stifled her sudden scream. She did not want anyone to get shot. She had worn the watch because it was inexpensive (valued at about ten dollars), and assumed it was not likely to catch anyone's attention.

Before long we were able to join her on the other side of the street. Relieved that she was alright, people on the street began dispersing, and we went into the beauty supply store. The shopping trip was shortened as we wanted to get back to the safety of the hotel. When Sister Luckett informed Pastor Luckett about the incident, he reprimanded us for leaving the hotel without him accompanying us. At any rate we had learned our lesson well, and did not make that mistake again.

Then it was time to plan the remaining days in Nairobi with Pastor Luckett, our host pastor, and the tour guides. The tour guides that would mainly assist us during our stay in Nairobi were introduced as Charles Olouch Apiyo and Josheph Ogembo.

First on the agenda was the purpose of our trip, a tent revival. We were informed that June was one of the rainy months in Kenya, and rain could possibly interfere with the scheduled revival. Still, we were optimistic, and later were taken to view the revival site in anticipation of services beginning on Tuesday.

Next up for discussion was how we would spend our down time when not in church. Arrangements were made for a safari (tour) into what we called the jungle, but it was actually the Nairobi National Park which was fenced in on three sides. After the park tour we would have dinner at the nearby prestigious Carnivore Restaurant. This restaurant served a variety of meats including wild cuisine (Zebra, Crocodile, Wildebeest, Ostrich, Wild Boar, Lamb, Pork, Beef, Chicken, and etcetera). We would also include a tour of special city landmarks and tribal dancing performances.

It was always quite strange that no matter where we went, or what pictures were being taken, Charles was always sitting or standing near me. Sister Mary Jones and Mother Amzie teased me about it a little lightheartedly. We concluded that there was nothing significant about the placement of Charles and me, and that it was merely coincidental.

In addition, no meaningful conversation had been exchanged between Charles and me, unless it related to the city in general. We also talked about Swahili, the general language of Kenya along with the mother tongue, or church related group discussions. Also, no matter where we went I felt a connection to the motherland.

One day as we were on an excursion to see a performance of tribal dances, I began videotaping scenery, grass, trees, and dirt. Pastor Luckett noticed and asked me if I was alright. I responded that I was alright, but that "I have been here before, and I just know the area." Pastor Luckett looked at me strangely, and then I realized that I had seen this same area in one of my prior dreams.

Also, in some of my former dreams I had married someone I associated as a brother. Even more perplexing was the fact that I was very satisfied being single. My children stated periodically that "I did not give men the time of day," and I did not. Why waste their time and mine too was really my motto? I dismissed the dreams at that time but now some of it was beginning to make sense.

In spite of the rain, the revival began. We knew the ground would be wet so we wore sneakers with our church clothes, and so did those in attendance. It was amazing to see how dedicated the worshippers were to making a joyful noise unto the Lord. They praised God as if they had no worries or cares. Even their testimonies regarding God's mercy shown them were so uplifting, in spite of hardships. They came from the nearby ghettos, and surrounding areas to hear the word of God and be blessed. I think they blessed us so much more than we blessed them.

No one had to prompt them to praise the Lord; it came naturally from grateful hearts. The musicians were so anointed, and the singers sometimes sang in their own dialect, which was so beautiful. Pastor Luckett preached the word of God under the anointing and I also ministered one night. Interpreters were present to translate the language into Swahili, even though most understood English. One had to really stay focused on the Lord as the lapse between your spoken word, and the interpreter's translation posed a challenge for those of us not accustomed to ministry of that sort.

Sometimes water had to be dipped from underneath the tent because of all the rain, but they came for church anyhow and still glorified the Lord. Yes, God is going to have a people that will praise Him in spite of! The prayer lines were lengthy but the worshippers left more encouraged than when they came.

The Thursday before our departure, I came to the hotel lobby a little early for church. The first person I saw was Charles, and he had come early to take us to church as well. We began talking about the revival and Kenya in general. I also shared with him how God had always given me a profound love for Africa.

He then began to tell me some things about our first meeting at the airport. Charles informed me that he had "noticed" me when they picked us up at the airport, and that we needed to talk. He mentioned that he had heard my statement in the van regarding the good driver. Also, when he saw my face in the rear view mirror, he knew God was about to do something special. The story overall is too lengthy for me to give additional details at this time, but I knew my life was in for some major changes.

Someone asked me "How do you fall in love with someone you do not even know?" I replied, "I had plenty of time, and dreams over the years." Sometimes love comes softly into the heart. I fell in love without even trying because Charles was the "man of my dreams." He had won my heart long before I met him in person. I had disregarded the earlier dreams because I could not understand how it was going to unfold with the mindset I had. Of all the places my mind could conceive, Africa was not one of them.

So yes, with Pastor Luckett's approval, we had one date that lasted about two hours, and we tried to discuss matters of importance from A to Z. He proposed the same night, and I said yes. We were married October 4, 1996 in Naroibi, Kenya.

It took a few years for all documentation to be approved by the Immigration and Naturalization Service office. Charles was eventually allowed entrance into the United States as a permanent resident in March 2000. During our marriage, he was a kind, hardworking, and tender-hearted gentleman. He had a wonderful sense of humor, and enjoyed engaging in political matters. The extras like flowers, candy and gifts were common everyday things. God blessed him to work well with his hands, and he could fix just about anything that was broken. He had been a pastor in Nairobi so I had no problem sharing the ministry with him.

One day before our marriage, I was sharing some things with Annie, my sister. She responded, "What if this is a well-laid trick of the Devil?" My reply was, "If I ever lose the husband I will always hold on to God."

Several happy years passed and I really loved that man. However, the marriage ended in divorce in 2007 (with me filing) for reasons I will not share at this time. I can say without a doubt that I kept my vows before God. Yet, when something or someone becomes a threat to your relationship with the Lord, it is time to make some adjustments. I knew that I could recover from a broken heart. I refused to let my circumstances dictate responses that could have caused me to forsake God, and possibly forfeit my freedom. So after two marriages and two divorces, I still have a healthy outlook on life, my sanity and salvation, as well as a God to glorify!

These are trying times, but the people of God must be tried in the fire, in order to come forth as pure gold. I firmly believe that when God looks at us, he should see a reflection of himself. So I say to you, **if you have to walk alone, stay with God!** A day of reckoning will come. Where do you want to spend eternity? Answer the question and live your life accordingly. Always acknowledge the Lord in all your ways and he will direct your path (Proverbs 3:6).

CHAPTER 13

HOLINESS AND
ENDANGERED SPECIES

On May 10, 2008, I attended a Baccalaureate
Service in support of one of Faith Temple's Youth
Department leaders, Winda Brown Carson. Winda
graduated and received degrees on the aforementioned date
from Tougaloo College. She had a double major, Early
Childhood Development and Child Development Education,
with a 3.75 grade point average (GPA).

While I was excited for her, my heart was grieved. I
observed among the multitude of those in attendance, how
far "the church has fallen" from standards of holiness, in
regards to apparel. I realize that nothing stays the same, and
that things are forever changing. "That Black Pentecostal
look" I referred to in Chapter 6 will not apply to every child
of God. However, I believe that there should be a distinct
difference in the way the "born again" people of God should
adorn themselves.

Of course, you can look fashionable (chic, stylish, trendy) without appearing trashy (cheap, unconcerned, shoddy). The Apostle Peter reminds us, "But ye are a chosen generation, a royal priesthood, an holy nation, a peculiar people; that ye should shew forth the praises of Him who hath called you out of darkness into His marvelous light." (1 Peter 2:9)

I agree that God is more concerned with the condition of the heart of an individual than He is with the outward appearance. However, there seems to be little regard to whom we represent primarily (Jesus, holiness). So what if "everybody is doing it." Will you be godly enough to be different? Before salvation, I embraced the tight-fitting clothing that outlined the contours of my body. It didn't get too short, the neckline too low or the clothing too transparent for me. Now that type of attire represented my worldly appetite, and I put them aside (abandoned) when I truly "got saved."

Paul cautions the church, "And be not conformed to this world: But be ye transformed by the renewing of your mind, that ye may prove what is that good, and acceptable, and perfect will of God." (Romans 12:2) I believe transformation includes the way we dress as well.

Nonetheless, what we often overlook is that if worldliness abides in the heart, it will exhibit itself in more than just clothing. It will show up in our points of compromise. How far will you go to blend in, be accepted by your peers or have "swag?"

Charlene was attempting to talk to me but I was listening to the voice of the Holy Ghost. I firmly believe that what concerns us, concerns God. I motioned to Charlene to wait a minute. Then I clearly heard the Spirit say, "Holiness as we once knew it is becoming an endangered species."

When a species becomes endangered it is in danger of extinction and that is certainly a great catastrophe. In the animal kingdom, extinction means all the members of an entire class are dead. Near the end of the movie and book, *"Last of the Mohicans,"* the old man was the last member of his tribe, and whenever he died, the tribe would be extinct.

The Lord knew I was disturbed by what I witnessed, and he sent that word especially for me, but I share it with you as well. It is up to the baptized, born again believers in Christ, to make sure holiness never becomes extinct. What can you do? Ask the Lord to teach you how to dress becoming to holiness, and let your behavior (manner of lifestyle) indicate that you represent Jesus.

During that process of revelation, the keynote speaker, Sheryl Lee Ralph, had been introduced. When I came back to reality, Ms. Ralph was saying, "We are an endangered species." I said to Charlene, "Did I just hear her say we are an endangered species?" She said, "Yes, you did." I then proceeded to share with her what the Holy Ghost had spoken.

The speaker related her statement in regards to character, and our Black male's manner of dressing (capitalizing on sagging pants). She delivered a stirring address while being totally realistic. I marveled at how close both "endangered species" statements related to each other. God is awesome!

We who profess a hope in Christ must align our lives with God's word. It is truly holiness or the lake that burns with fire and brimstone (referred to as hell). There is no "holding place" between heaven and the lake of fire after death for mankind to repent, and obtain God's mercy and grace. If so, this could possibly make an individual fit for the kingdom.

John, the revelator, tells us plainly how we will appear before the judgment throne of God. He states, "He that is unjust, let him be unjust still: and he which is filthy, let him be filthy still: and he that is righteous, let him be righteous still: and he that is holy, let him be holy still." (Revelations 22:11)

The time is now! For John also states, "Search the scriptures; for in them ye think ye have eternal life: and they are they which testify of me. And ye will not come to me that ye might have life." (John 5:39-40). Holidays, celebrations, or vacations are not days that exempt us from living godly lives.

The message is the same; prepare to meet thy God for pay day is coming sooner than we think. Let's get holiness off the "endangered species" listing. Pass the message on as God's mercy is extended unto us daily; let us not take it lightly. Think about it!

Chapter 14

SPECIAL RECOGNITION

I have truly been blessed by the Lord to have people that have sown good seeds into my life in ways that cannot be numbered. A mere "thank you" will never be sufficient. Neither time nor space will allow me to mention all the names. Just know that God will not forget your labor of love. Below are just a few individuals I would like to give special recognition to:

Helen Miller Brown, You are a blessing to me! You are more than a sister-in-law; you are an inspiration. You have always been there with a word in due season and a smile. Thanks for your continual prayers and help through the years. I know it is the God in you. I love you dearly.

Leora Poston, You've prayed, pushed and prophesied. I had to find my place in God, and you were the Mid-wife overseeing the birth. You are more than a friend, you are my sister, and I love you.

Dessie Hall, Wife of my adopted father, the late Elder Joe Hall, Sr., thanks for welcoming me to the family along with Jalisha, Joe and Moses. I love you and all my Tupelo, Mississippi, daughters.

Patricia Hill and Sara Allen, You have prayed and fasted countless times on my behalf, and the Faith Temple Ministry. God will not forget your labor of love as prayer warriors. I thank God for you and love you dearly.

Christopher "Peter" Rainey, Michael and Maurice Hathorne, John "Sam" Kennedy, and Elmo Ferguson, Thanks for helping to mentor my sons by taking them hunting and fishing with your team. You were "A part of the village" and I appreciate you.

Cathy Harmon and Lahoma Johnson, Thank you for your assistance with Lili during her teenage years. I am truly indebted to you. I love you.

Terry and Emma Greer, Helen Clark, Gwendolyn Leflore, Coleman T. Harris and Charlie, I appreciate your words of encouragement. Thanks for "believing in me."

Leake County School District, Carthage, Mississippi, (present and past Superintendents, Assistant Superintendents, School Board Members and Thomastown School principals) I have been employed for the past 23 ½ years with the district and I am grateful. Thank you.

*   *   *

In Remembrance

My Faith Temple Church Family has nurtured me in so many ways. The following members of the church family are now deceased but their memories live on in my heart. I acknowledge that many of those faithful warriors not only sowed good seeds into my life, but helped to shape the Faith Temple Pentecostal Church Mission. They blessed this ministry with their labors of love, finances and spiritual gifts. Their service was rendered to the Glory of God, my life was touched, and the ministry was enhanced. In remembrance of the following:

Mable Cottrell Adams
James & Georgia Ashford
Jaqueline Ashford
Martha Ann Ashford
Robert & Florence Barksdale
Evangelist Daisy Della Barry
Fannie Bowie
Willie James Brown
L.C. & Mayzell Cooper
Roy & Troy Dotson
Annie Doris Ferguson
George "Larry" Fleming
Hattie Mae Fondren
Dorothy Gilbert
Sam Hazley
Alice Ingram
Annie Bowie Johnson
Greg Thomas Jones
Clinton & Adline Knox
Odie D. Lee
S. D. & Annie Mae Leflore
Pastor David Luckett
Louise McDonald

Luevenia McDonald
Edna Merredith
Mae Eunice Miller
Cynthia Alston Mosley
Leslie King Newman
George Arthur Rainey
Annie Jackson Sanlin
Pastor Lillie B. Sanlin
Annie Ruth Simmons
Elder Billy & Barbara Sparkman
Magnolia Brown Stewart
Cornelius Washington
Willie Mae Welch
Loutema Wellmaker
Pastor Gloria Woodard